COACHES GUIDE TO
TIME
MANAGEMENT

ACEP Level 2 Sport Science Courses

ACEP Level 2 sport science courses are available to accompany the following texts:

Coaches Guide to Sport Law by Gary Nygaard and Thomas H. Boone. The authors explain a coach's legal responsibilities in easy to understand terms and give practical advice for improving standards of care and safety for athletes.

Coaches Guide to Time Management by Charles Kozoll. This innovative text shows coaches how to improve their self-organization and how to avoid the harmful effects of stress by controlling the pressures inherent in many coaching programs.

Coaches Guide to Sport Physiology by Brian Sharkey leads coaches step-by-step through the development of fitness-training programs suitable for their sport and for the athletes they coach.

Coaches Guide to Sport Injuries by David Bergeron and Holly Wilson gives coaches information on injury prevention and on the immediate treatment and follow-up care for common athletic injuries.

Coaches Guide to Teaching Sport Skills by Bob Christina uses practical coaching examples to take coaches through the teaching/learning process and offers coaches valuable advice for improving their teaching effectiveness.

Coaches Guide to Sport Psychology by Rainer Martens presents information on motivation, communication, stress management, the use of mental imagery, and other fascinating topics for enhancing coach-athlete relationships and for stimulating improved sport performances.

Each course consists of a *Coaches Guide*, a *Study Guide*, and a *Workbook*. ACEP certification is awarded for successful course completion. For more information about these courses, write to:

ACEP Level 2
Box 5076
Champaign, IL 61820
(217)351-5076

COACHES GUIDE TO TIME MANAGEMENT

A publication for the
American Coaching Effectiveness Program
Level 2 Sport Science Curriculum

Charles E. Kozoll, PhD
University of Illinois

HUMAN KINETICS PUBLISHERS, INC.
Champaign, Illinois

Library of Congress Cataloging in Publication Data

Kozoll, Charles E.
    Coaches guide to time management.

    Bibliography: p.
    Includes index.
    1. Coaching (Athletics) 2. Coaches
(Athletics)—Time management. I. Title.
GV711.K69   1985   796'.07'7   85-793
ISBN 0-931250-97-8

Developmental Editor: Stephen C. Jefferies
Production Director: Sara Chilton
Copy Editor: Olga Murphy
Typesetter: Yvonne Sergent
Text Layout: Lezli Harris
Illustrator: Jerry Barrett
Cover Design and Layout: Jack W. Davis
Printed by: BookCrafters

ISBN: 0-931250-97-8
Copyright © 1985 by Charles E. Kozoll

Printed in the United States of America

10 9 8 7 6 5 4 3 2 1

Human Kinetics Publishers, Inc.
Box 5076, Champaign, IL 61820

For the Kozolls in my life,
Joan, Richard, Scott

Contents

Acknowledgments

Conducting time management workshops and writing about this same subject are two distinctly different activities. Participants at workshops can and should ask for clarification if an idea or approach is not clear. In the lonely activity of writing, an author has to depend on editors for clarification.

As this book was conceptualized and prepared, I have been exceedingly fortunate to work with three capable and supportive editors. Rainer Martens did much to encourage improved organization and writing. Margery Brandfon was instrumental in turning ideas into well-thought-out chapters and sentences. Stephen Jefferies provided insightful suggestions for improving the clarity and organization of the book. All their efforts are deeply appreciated.

Lynn Padilla and Cindy Curtiss were faced with my curious scrawl as well as numerous revisions. Their assistance and fine work were most valuable to completion of this project.

Finally, a number of coaches contributed their ideas on realistic time management to this book. Several suggested the value of using a few techniques each day to accomplish goals and to keep pressure within limits. I thank them for their assistance.

Introduction

As a young college student stationed in East Africa years ago, I was introduced to "the Mixture." It was a unique remedy for an upset stomach, developed by a Scottish physician who had served many years in Sub-Saharan Africa. Upon first treating me, this doctor prescribed a medicine to which he referred as *the* mixture, not *a* mixture. His irritable response to my inquiry about his choice of words was, "What you're getting, sonny, is *the* mixture that I've worked on for many years. It will take care of whatever ails you and can also be used to repair broken plates or patch holes in the screens around your house." The mixture did work on my stomach, although I never tried it out on plates or screens.

As a result, the word *the* signifying *one* way or *one* prescription has made me nervous ever since. My interest in time management has renewed this skepticism about single routes to solving often complex individual or group problems.

In preparing this book, I spoke to coaches in a variety of different sports and settings across the country. I examined these coaches' public statements and also collected many athletes' comments about effective coaches. The results of this investigation have led me to suggest routes for effective time management for coaches. I offer no prescriptions, but suggest basic organizing approaches which you can fit to your own coaching style, setting, and sport.

Coaches tend to be busy, energetic people, willing to accept many responsibilities. They are expected to manage complex athletic programs and produce talented athletes in a highly pressured environment. Many coaches are volunteers who must juggle coaching with their careers and families. Frequently, they find themselves running frantically from task to task, trying to accomplish too much and very often accomplishing too little. Left with no time for themselves and for their friends and families, these coaches burn out mentally and physically.

The *Coaches Guide to Time Management* is for busy and overburdened coaches who want to control the pressure sports place on them. Time management is a means to an end, not an end in itself. The coaches who helped me develop this book emphasize that point. Effective time management will improve the quality of your life. As you read this book, carefully consider the contribution improved self-organization could make to the success of your athletic program, to the development of your athletes, and to the enjoyment you derive from coaching.

The book is divided into two parts. Part 1 challenges you to examine your own time management effectiveness and also presents some examples of the problems coaches who manage time poorly experience. The basic elements of time management are explained, and coaches are encouraged to critically examine the organization of their own coaching programs. Organizational concerns common to all programs are discussed and many suggestions offered for possible improvements.

Part 2 contains examples of time management techniques in practice. Case studies of full-time, part-time, and volunteer coaches illustrate different attitudes toward improving personal effectiveness. These coaches reveal highly personalized management systems which match their own unique personality characteristics. The book concludes with a review of recommended time management techniques and offers suggestions for developing and maintaining your own time management system. A Time Management Course, which uses this book and an accompanying study guide, is available from the American Coaching Effectiveness Program (ACEP).

PART 1
Managing Time

Time is best managed when people understand why time is important and how it can easily be managed. Part 1 of this book will explain both the "why's" and the "how's" of managing time.

Chapter 1 shows what happens when individuals and their organizations manage time poorly. The material comes, in part, from participants in time management seminars who reviewed their frantic days and saw how little they accomplished. In this chapter, you will meet two coaches who hurt themselves and others through their poor management of time. Although they operate very differently, these coaches prevent themselves from coaching effectively, making accomplishment difficult for both their athletes and assistants. The coaches are fictionalized, but their methods represent those of coaches I have interviewed and observed. The chapter concludes by introducing you to the ACORN environment, a chaotic environment which makes it difficult for people to reach their potential and work together as a cohesive, effective group.

In chapter 2 you are encouraged to analyze your own time use and evaluate your ACORN creating tendencies. Methods are presented for examining your effectiveness as a time manager and for identifying areas which would benefit from improved self-organization.

Effective time management depends on the combination of two critical factors: direction and control. Chapter 3 outlines how to establish direction by setting realistic goals, priorities, and limits for your athletic programs. Two key techniques for control are discussed in chapter 4: concentration and distress management. Maintaining control over coaching distractions and pressures will enable you to focus attention on improving the quality of your program.

Successful and happy coaches who use time wisely have helped me prepare this book. The secret of their success is organization. In conversations with coaches, I discovered many of them had unique systems which contributed to daily accomplishment and which kept pressure under control. In Part 2, you will meet some of these coaches and complete the development of your own personal recipe for effective time management.

Time management is an ongoing, continuous process as is illustrated in the following chart. The steps in the chart correspond to chapters in this book. This chart will appear at the beginning of each chapter to remind you of the developmental cycle for improving your skills of time management.

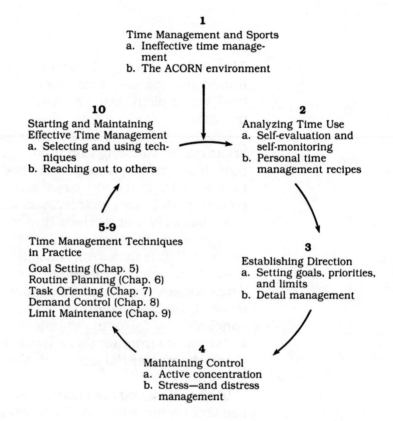

1

Time Management and Sports
a. Ineffective time management
b. The ACORN environment

10

Starting and Maintaining Effective Time Management
a. Selecting and using techniques
b. Reaching out to others

2

Analyzing Time Use
a. Self-evaluation and self-monitoring
b. Personal time management recipes

5-9

Time Management Techniques in Practice

Goal Setting (Chap. 5)
Routine Planning (Chap. 6)
Task Orienting (Chap. 7)
Demand Control (Chap. 8)
Limit Maintenance (Chap. 9)

3

Establishing Direction
a. Setting goals, priorities, and limits
b. Detail management

4

Maintaining Control
a. Active concentration
b. Stress—and distress management

Chapter 1
Time Management and Sports

1
Time Management and Sports
a. **Ineffective time management**
b. **The ACORN environment**

10
Starting and Maintaining
Effective Time Management
a. Selecting and using techniques
b. Reaching out to others

2
Analyzing Time Use
a. Self-evaluation and
  self-monitoring
b. Personal time
  management recipes

5-9
Time Management Techniques
in Practice

Goal Setting (Chap. 5)
Routine Planning (Chap. 6)
Task Orienting (Chap. 7)
Demand Control (Chap. 8)
Limit Maintenance (Chap. 9)

3
Establishing Direction
a. Setting goals, priorities,
  and limits
b. Detail management

4
Maintaining Control
a. Active concentration
b. Stress—and distress
  management

**MANAGING
TIME**

Everyone manages time—some well, some not so well. Poor time management has an adverse effect not only on the individual coach, but on all those who come into contact with the coach. Assistant coaches, trainers, managers, athletes, and others involved in the program suffer the consequences of poor management in unpleasant and sometimes disastrous ways. Effective time management often means the difference between a successful and an unsuccessful athletic program.

To illustrate this point, let us meet two coaches who manage their time poorly and see how they affect themselves and others. Although these two individuals coach full time, effective time management is no less vital for part-time or volunteer coaches. In many ways, managing time is even more important for volunteer coaches who must juggle coaching responsibilities with a regular job.

Two Poor Time Managers

Sarah Stiel and Frank Adams are coaches at the same midwestern university. Each has a unique way of organizing an athletic program. Sarah spends her life on the run, always available and always willing to accept new responsibilities. In contrast, Frank usually wanders around and procrastinates until only a few days before a game. Then, with time running out, he frantically attempts to complete his team preparations. The environments Sarah and Frank create are unpleasant, both for themselves and for others. Working under these conditions stifles the potential of each coach, their assistants, and athletes. Let us examine in detail how Sarah and Frank manage (or mismanage) a typical Monday.

Sarah's Race Against the Clock

Sarah usually arrives at her office early, anticipating a busy day. Once she opens her door, it stays open all day except for three occasions: when she goes out for a brief lunch, during practice, and when she leaves early in the evening. Sarah is convinced she must always be accessible, regardless of her assignment schedule. The open door is a signal that others may interrupt her at any time.

During the morning, the open door invites passersby to drop in for visits, to make requests, or to ask questions. Sarah never asks them to come back later, no matter how trivial the conversation. She is willing to talk or listen all morning and will even sometimes leave her office to chat with others in the corridor.

About midmorning an assistant coach drops in to ask Sarah for help with an assignment: An inventory report of the team's equipment is due by the end of the week. The assistant has been repeatedly instructed on how to do this task but does not enjoy counting and making lists. After listening to a few of the assistant's excuses, Sarah agrees to help. She clips the stack of inventory forms together and places them at the top of an already tall pile of papers sitting on her "get to" table, which is the house for one tall stack of papers of theoretically high-priority activities. On another small desk and two tables, Sarah has piled forms, correspondence, announcements, and brochures. Sarah frequently wastes time looking for lost papers because she never sorts the important items from the unimportant ones. Today, she hunts for two letters of interest from prospective recruits, as well as for two competition registration forms, deadlines for which are fast approaching.

The Pace Accelerates

After the assistant leaves, Sarah tries to work, keeping her door open. The visits cease, but now the phone begins to ring. Two calls heighten Sarah's anxiety level. The first is from a friend who asks Sarah to arrange main speakers for next spring's state conference. Despite the likelihood of a hectic spring schedule, Sarah agrees to help her friend. The second call is from the athletic director who wants to know if Sarah has finished the United Way collections. Controlling her panic,

Sarah assures the chairman that she is nearly done but chides herself, "Got to get on that!"

Without further outside distractions, Sarah remembers another priority task—writing letters to two high school athletes. If she does not do this soon, they will think she is not interested. After 10 minutes of searching, she finds their letters and clears some space on her desk to write friendly replies. Midway through the second paragraph, she remembers she forgot to register for the two-state classic. Sarah stops writing the letters and makes three long distance calls to get forms. In fact, these were sent to her 2 weeks ago and lay in one of the stacks on the crowded table. In her panic, Sarah does not stop to think whether or not she already has the forms; she only remembers this fact after $10 worth of long distance calls and an hour of nervous activity.

At 11:00 a.m., Sarah, already frantic, begins to prepare for a noontime speech to a local athletic booster club. Instead of concentrating, Sarah interrupts her own thoughts by anticipating phone calls and by thinking of her other projects. With a half page of hastily scrawled notes in hand, Sarah rushes out at 11:40 a.m. Giving an already overburdened department secretary the blank two-state classic registration forms, she implores her to complete them. She leaves the building, shouting the instructions: "Use the same information as last year! Need them this afternoon! Thanks!" Rushing out the door, Sarah fails to notice the secretary's anger at having to bail her out again.

Driving to the luncheon, Sarah starts thinking about practice, and in the relative calm, she finally figures out how to solve a major problem. She intends to write down her thoughts before lunch but gets caught up in various conversations and forgets yet another good idea.

After the speech, several boosters congratulate Sarah on her presentation and express confidence in her ability to turn the team around. What Sarah does not hear as she hurries out is their whispered comments about her tense and preoccupied appearance.

Nonexistent Planning

At 1:30, Sarah returns to her office, determined to devote the remaining 2 hours to planning the 3:30 practice. Although her schedule is clear, Sarah has barely sat down at her desk when a troubled athlete appears at her door with a problem that cannot wait. Before Sarah can respond, the athlete sits down and starts explaining the difficulty—one Sarah should have known about and taken precautions to prevent. During this meeting, the department secretary interrupts, saying, "Coach, they have changed the forms for the two-state classic. The committee wants new information, and you are the only one who has it." The secretary leaves the partially completed forms on Sarah's desk with a note that they are already overdue *and* the team will have to pay a late registration fee. As the athlete explains her problem, Sarah is wondering how she will explain the late registration to the athletic director. With her mind going in a dozen different directions at once, Sarah hears only about a third of what the athlete is saying, and this is evident in the inadequate response she gives to the athlete's request for advice.

When the athlete leaves, Sarah rushes off to practice, which turns out to be a complete disaster. Players stand around with nothing to do and joke or just play on their own. Two assistant coaches, if not continually coming up for directions, try to improvise. Head coach, Sarah, once a superior athlete and a master game strategist, runs up and down the practice field, shouting hastily conceived instructions. At first, her lack of planning confuses the players and coaches, then later leaves them frustrated. Practice ends with the athletes feeling dejected and ill-prepared, and lacking confidence for their next game.

Tuesday, Wednesday, and Thursday prove to be no better for Sarah. In fact, as the week progresses, these days turn out to be even worse as Sarah grows increasingly more tense and frantic. Because Sarah is the leader of the team, her attitude is highly contagious. Coaches and players snap at each other, culminating with the team losing on Saturday to opponents they should have beaten.

Frank's Too Leisurely Pace

While Sarah represents one extreme of poor time management, Frank represents the other. On the surface, Frank appears calmer than Sarah, but he is equally disorganized. Frank is convinced that he does his best work under pressure. However, he does not understand how his assistant coaches and players feel about last-minute efforts. Let us carefully look at one of Frank's typical weeks to see how he manages time.

A Slow Start

Frank shakes his head with a combination of awe and amusement as he watches Sarah run. That frantic pace is not for him. He prefers a more relaxed approach, at least at the beginning of the week. On Monday, he briefly reviews the last game and decides what needs to be done at practices. No immediate decision is taken, however, because Monday's and Tuesday's practices are always the same: The team works on its own with a little guidance from the two assistant coaches. Frank wanders up and down the sidelines watching.

Before practice, Frank occupies himself with an assortment of interests and distractions. He skims articles, takes a long coffee break with friends, and works out for an hour before lunch. After lunch, he looks at some letters and forms but decides to put them aside until the next day. Frank does not notice that the department secretary has underlined a deadline.

Before leaving for practice, Frank reads through a new equipment catalogue. "I'd never get money for some of this stuff," he thinks. "The athletic director would never agree." While daydreaming about the improvement this equipment would make to the team's performance, an assistant coach interrupts him, wanting to discuss the team's next opponent before practice. "Let's hold off until tomorrow," Frank replies.

His lack of interest is obvious which discourages the assistant from making future suggestions.

The assistant coach is not the only one to notice Frank's apathy. Many of the athletes wonder why Frank even bothers coming to practice until Thursday when he finally begins to show concern. Other faculty members marvel that even though Frank is in the middle of a season, he can routinely enjoy leisurely lunches. One enthusiastic team booster had to call three times to remind Frank about two prize prospects visiting this week's game. Because Frank never returns the calls, the booster himself makes arrangements for the visit but decides not to help out again because his efforts are not appreciated.

Early in the week Frank always has time to drop in on the assistant coaches to chat or to propose ideas and new work for them. These conversations end with, "Why don't you look into that?", leaving the assistants uncertain whether to treat the comment as a suggestion or as a firm request. Weekly staff meetings have this same nondirective and indeterminate quality. Frank always seems more interested in proposing ideas than in dealing with the practical preparations for upcoming games. He loathes details and considers such questions as what time the bus leaves trivial. Unfortunately, his assistants can't make certain decisions, and Frank won't.

When he is calm and bored at the beginning of the week, Frank has a habit of interrupting others in the athletic department. He considers dropping in on Sarah a favor to her, thinking he is helping her to relax from her frenetic pace. Frank interrupts secretaries, graduate assistants, equipment managers, and ticket sellers. Unfortunately, because Frank is a head coach, few are bold enough to ask him to come back later.

**First Pro-
crastination,
Then Pressure**

Frank follows the same relaxed pace Tuesday and Wednesday, but early Thursday morning, his adrenalin begins to flow. Saturday is not so far away and the extent of what remains to be done suddenly dawns on him. On Thursday and Friday, Frank starts to resemble Sarah.

"Why didn't you tell me about that form?" he complains to the department secretary after receiving a call about it. "Weren't you supposed to get me information on our opponents?" he asks the assistant coach. "You guys won't get anywhere with that attitude!" he yells to some players who make mistakes running a new play.

Thursday's and Friday's practices are active, intense, and often confusing to players. Although Frank is an able coach, he delivers his ideas too quickly, leaving the players little time to absorb the suggestions. On Friday, Frank and his assistant coach try to catch up with last-minute details before the game in vain. Luckily, it is a home game, or the athletes may have had to find their own hotel rooms. At one away game, the team did leave several bags of equipment behind because no one knew who was supposed to bring them.

In order to make the necessary arrangements, Frank has to plead for special favors "just one more time." Although he must do some photocopying outside the university and, therefore, at twice the cost, Frank only shrugs his shoulders. He has the same reaction upon learning what happened to the two prize prospects, whose housing arrangements were made by the booster. These young athletes are given sideline made by the booster. These young athletes are given sideline passes for the game and a short campus tour with one of the new assistant coaches. Frank does not bother to meet the young athletes, and the prospects leave campus on Sunday convinced they will not return to this university.

Frank's team wins on Saturday. Three key players on the opposing team were injured the previous week and their replacements made enough errors to compensate for Frank's poor preparation. "We didn't win, they lost," the assistant coach mumbles. Meanwhile, Frank congratulates the team, adding that they do their best work under pressure. Although Frank notices the locker room is strangely silent after his last comment, he considers this only momentarily and leaves.

Poor Time Management

Let us review Frank's management of the weekly coaching schedule. The week begins at a too leisurely pace, then finishes with frantic last-minute preparation. Because Frank believes he works better under pressure, he does not notice a problem with his time management. In contrast, Sarah believes she cannot change her frantic days to more controlled ones. Her door is open and cannot be closed. She feels obliged to take on more and reacts to events on a day-to-day basis instead of being guided by a plan of action. Tragically, the potential of both coaches remains unrealized because of their poor time management. In addition, their actions create environments which athletes, assistants, and supporters find stressful and unpleasant. These elements can be simply summarized with one acronym: ACORN.

THE ACORN SETTING

ACORN is an acronym describing the environment Sarah and Frank create for the people around them. Those who must work in this setting—coaches, assistant coaches, athletes, secretaries, boosters, and many others, gradually become *Aggressive*, *Compulsive*, *Ornery*, and finally, *Really Nutty*.

The Effects of Poor Time Management

If we look closer at Sarah's Monday, we can see just how many people she affected by her poor time management.

1. The friend who asked Sarah to find a speaker, for it is doubtful Sarah will successfully complete this.

2. The athletic director whose concern over the United Fund collections was left unresolved.

3. The two prospective athletes who are left to wonder if Sarah is interested in them. They probably will not show any further interest in attending Sarah's university.

4. The booster club members who notice Sarah's tenseness and begin to wonder if she is the best person for the job.

5. The organizers of the two-state classic who will probably receive incorrectly filled-out forms.

6. The overworked secretary, who was asked to do another last-minute salvaging job—something she will be increasingly less willing to do in the future.

7. The athlete who looked to Sarah for help, yet barely received a third of Sarah's attention—a fact the athlete may have mentioned to other teammates.

8. The entire team of potentially successful athletes and assistant coaches, who are frustrated by a lack of direction.

9. Everyone else whose life Sarah has made harder through her ineffectiveness. Eventually, her methods will create such bad feelings that she will not find any support when she most needs it.

Frank has a similar effect on others in the athletic department. These include the following:

1. The department secretary who is criticized for not pointing out the deadline—something she did do earlier in the week.

2. The enthusiastic assistant who wanted to share information about the team's next opponents and was turned away.

3. The athletes who are frustrated by Frank's lack of concern early in the week and by his unrealistic expectations at the last minute.

4. The team booster who wanted to help but whose efforts were ignored—he won't help again.

5. Assistant coaches who are never certain what action to take following Frank's proposals and who are frustrated by Frank's inability to make decisions.

6. Sarah and others in the athletic department whose work Frank interrupts whenever he feels bored.

Frank deceives himself by believing he does his best work under pressure. Sometimes he is lucky, and his team still wins. But with or without luck, Frank frustrates everyone in contact with him. Procrastinating early in the week wastes valuable thinking and planning time. Frank lets his own time evaporate, and he interrupts others who are trying to do their own jobs.

On Thursdays and Fridays, when he and his team must cram a week's worth of preparation into 2 frantic days, Frank makes mistakes and forgets important details. Although Frank claims to work best under pressure, he begins blaming others for what they were unable to do because of his procrastination.

Sarah's and Frank's assistants and athletes want to contribute to the program's success, and all have valuable contributions to make. Unfortunately, Frank and Sarah do not make use of the information, talent, and advice available. Their lack of sensitivity erodes the loyalty and support of others. In short, Sarah and Frank make life miserable for other people; they create ACORN environments and fail to consider how their actions affect others. They do not realize that time is a collective resource which must be used intelligently for the benefit of all, not something for their personal use only.

**Time as a
Collective Resource**

Time management techniques are often prescribed to help individuals improve themselves. But individual improvement is often dependent on the cooperation of others. Efforts to improve time management may fail without the understanding and endorsement of your family and colleagues. Coaches often find themselves in situations where they suffer the effects of other coaches' disorganization. The disorganized behavior of Sarah and Frank affected many people negatively, creating a chaotic and aimless working environment. If you, too, are a poor time manager, you are probably reducing the productivity and success of others in your program.

Coaches manage environments. Regardless of the sport or whether you are coaching "peewees" or collegiate athletes, you are responsible for creating and maintaining a *healthy working environment*. This includes a well-planned program with a clear sense of direction, realistic limits, and a climate that encourages individual and group productivity. In other words, you must strive to create an atmosphere in which people enjoy working together.

Before continuing to discuss how you can ensure that your athletic program has direction, limits, and a calm but productive climate, let's examine the management problems contributing to an ACORN environment.

**MANAGEMENT
PROBLEMS
CONTRIBUTING
TO AN ACORN
ENVIRONMENT**

Research has indicated that poor time managers generally suffer from one or more of the following management problems:

- Relying on "Mythical Time"
- Underestimating Demands On Time
- Task Creep
- Task Hopping
- Ignoring Reality

In the next section we examine each of these management problems in more detail. You will then be able to reexamine your own management skills and avoid the mistakes Sarah and Frank made.

Relying on "Mythical Time"

This management problem leads to putting off assignments in the mistaken belief you will later have a larger block of uninterrupted time available in which to complete your assignments. Sarah believed she would have 1:30 to 3:30 p.m. to plan the afternoon practice. Her reliance on free time that did not exist—mythical time—lulled her into thinking she had plenty of time. Consequently, she allowed herself to be overly accessible in the morning. The "real" time she had on Monday morning could have been valuably used. It is easy to believe that you will have more time in the future than you do at present. Unfortunately, when the future arrives, you quickly discover that this belief was indeed a myth.

By relying on mythical time, Sarah gave away her real time. At 1:30, her 2 free hours were eaten away by legitimate demands: an athlete with a problem and forms that urgently needed to be filled out. Sarah knows her mornings will be frequently interrupted by visitors and telephone calls and encourages these interruptions by keeping her door open. Sarah does not recognize that she will always have interruptions, both in the morning and in the afternoon. Instead of leaving large, important tasks for later, she should start taking care of them *immediately*. She could divide complex, high-priority tasks into smaller, more manageable pieces. She could make one major activity—such as planning practice—the morning's single focus. With this approach, Sarah would depend less on mythical time and give priorities the immediate attention they deserve.

In a similar way, Frank put off any form of planning or organization until the end of the week. He failed to recognize that it was impossible to complete team preparations successfully in the time he made available. He avoided high-priority tasks early in the week instead of giving them immediate attention. The week ended in panic, creating a stressful situation for athletes, coaches, and others associated with Frank's program.

Underestimating Demands on Time

Underestimating the demands on your time results from not recognizing how much time you really control each day. Problems arise because you take on more than you realistically expect to do in the limited time available. Sarah actually controls only a third of her day, whereas she mistakenly believes she controls far more. Sarah makes the mistake of taking on too much for the time she has available.

As a coach, Sarah must respond to the legitimate demands others make on her time accounting for two-thirds of her day. Sarah could accomplish more if she recognized how much time she actually controlled, as well as how much she cannot control. She could divide her day roughly into thirds, with the third she does control being used for high-priority tasks, such as planning practice and filling out required forms. The second third could be allocated for legitimate interruptions and requests, such as athletes needing to discuss problems, parents wishing to discuss their child's performance, or other coaches needing an impromptu meeting to discuss new ideas or to resolve problems. The remaining third of her time could then be used for unexpected crises, such as tracking down a missing equipment shipment, taking care of an injured athlete, holding an emergency staff meeting, or finding new hotel reservations when the old ones are lost.

Sarah treats interruptions as just that—as intrusions into her ideally uncluttered, mythical time. Some interruptions, however, are not intrusions but are a part of coaching. Sarah should expect interruptions and make time to deal with them.

Setting priorities is a key element in the effective use of time. Recruiting new athletes and planning for practice are priority activities and should receive priority attention. Discussing a problem with an athlete should receive complete, rather than half-hearted attention. No matter how effective Sarah's planning and organization, she must learn to live with the unexpected. If Sarah recognized this, she would realistically evaluate her ability to accept new assignments.

Task Creep

Task creep is the problem of failing to complete immediate tasks before agreeing to do more. If Sarah stayed within the third of time she controls each day, she would carry a lighter load of truly essential activities and could integrate legitimate requests and crises more easily. Unfortunately, because Sarah does not recognize how little time she actually has, she fills her schedule with too many nonessential tasks. As Sarah continues to accept more and more assignments, she forgets what she already has to do: Sarah agrees to help with an inventory that is her assistant's responsibility; she agrees to find a speaker for next year's state conference; and she agrees to finish the United Way collections immediately, without requesting any assistance.

The results of task creep are obvious: (a) Sarah is forced to lie to the athletic director; (b) she wastes time (hers and the secretary's) and money on the two-state classic forms; (c) she gives an ill-prepared speech to the booster club; (d) she listens half-heartedly to a troubled athlete; and (e) she holds haphazard, discouraging practices.

Controlling task creep requires more frequent use of the word NO. Many people find this a hard word to use. But hard is not impossible, and lightening the load will do much to eliminate an ACORN environment.

Task Hopping

Task hopping is the result of poor concentration. This is caused by too many tasks and too little sense of priority. Task hopping coaches are easily identified: They stare into space; they look around and are always searching to find a form or a manual; they wait in anticipation of a telephone call or a visit; and they listen to others or perform one task while thinking about others.

Both Sarah and Frank are task hoppers. Frank flips through some important forms, then puts them down to skim practice plans. He develops then drops ideas and does not complete anything. Sarah starts one task, interrupting it to start another. She thinks up good ideas but loses them because she does not write them down. Both Frank and Sarah task hop by creating unnecessary interruptions—Sarah by being too accessible and Frank by procrastinating.

Ignoring Reality

Ignoring reality is perhaps the hardest problem to correct because you must examine yourself with a critical and objective eye. Ignoring reality is ignoring the fact that certain personal traits and beliefs *undermine* rather than enhance an athletic program. Sarah ignores reality by clinging to the belief she must always be accessible. Her accessibility and unrealistic willingness to serve, prevent her from attending to important work.

Frank's belief that he works best under pressure means that he spends 3 days bothering everyone else and 2 panicky days making errors, forgetting important details, and blaming others for his poor preparation. Ignoring reality also means ignoring the effects of these personal traits on others. Sarah and Frank are responsible for overburdening already swamped assistants, letting down friends and supporters, and hurting others' feelings.

SUMMARY AND RECOM-MENDATIONS

The coaches described in this chapter experienced problems familiar to all poor time managers. Sarah Stiel attempted too much and in trying to meet all her responsibilities, failed to attend to the most important tasks. Frank Adams confused and frustrated his athletes and assistants because of his insensitivity and his tendency to avoid responsibilities until the last minute. Both coaches suffered because of a lack of planning and self-organization. These managerial behaviors are frequently the source of organizational problems. The potential of the two coaches, their assistants, and their athletes was not realized. Effective time management is critical to the success of all athletic programs. Therefore, as a coach you should recognize the following:

1. Time is a collective resource. Coaches' management of *environments* affects how others manage time and influences the achievement of individual and program success.

2. By mismanaging your own time, you create stressful working environments for your colleagues.

3. You may create ACORN environments: climates in which people become Aggressive, Compulsive, Ornery, and Really Nutty.

4. Five management problems contribute to the development of an ACORN environment. These include (a) relying on mythical time, (b) underestimating demands on time, (c) task creep, (d) task hopping, and (e) ignoring reality.

Coaches with poor management skills can have a disastrous effect on an athletic program. The next chapter will take a closer look at time and will examine your effectiveness as a time manager.

Chapter 2
Analyzing Time Use

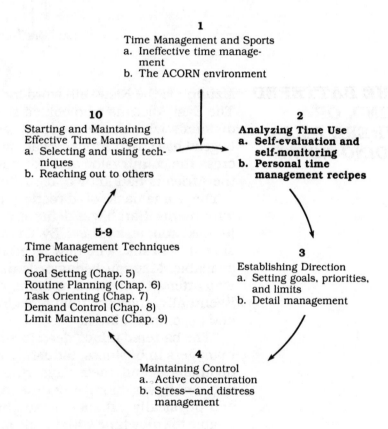

1
Time Management and Sports
a. Ineffective time management
b. The ACORN environment

10
Starting and Maintaining Effective Time Management
a. Selecting and using techniques
b. Reaching out to others

2
Analyzing Time Use
a. **Self-evaluation and self-monitoring**
b. **Personal time management recipes**

5-9
Time Management Techniques in Practice

Goal Setting (Chap. 5)
Routine Planning (Chap. 6)
Task Orienting (Chap. 7)
Demand Control (Chap. 8)
Limit Maintenance (Chap. 9)

3
Establishing Direction
a. Setting goals, priorities, and limits
b. Detail management

4
Maintaining Control
a. Active concentration
b. Stress—and distress management

SELF-EVALUATING

The last chapter described some of the problems created by poor time management. Sarah Stiel and Frank Adams did not appreciate the impact their ineffective time management had on others working in the athletic program. Neither recognized the problems caused by their poor organization, believing that these problems were beyond their control. To be an effective time manager, you must first understand the extent to which outcomes are dependent on *your* organizational skills. Failing to accept this responsibility inevitably creates management problems.

THE BATTERED MIND, OR WHERE AM I GOING NOW?

Mzungu is the Kiswahili word for anyone with a white skin. The East Africans who coined the word say it describes individuals who wander around with no apparent direction. Legend has it that Africans watched European explorers crisscross the countryside and "discover" lakes and mountains the Africans had known about for centuries.

The same lack of direction is common in many environments. Sarah was definitely mzungu on Monday as she jumped from task to task. By Thursday mzungu behavior had spread to Frank, who now faced too many tasks in the time available. Mzungu behavior is displayed by many coaches who attempt too much or fail to control their environment. Eventually, these mzungus begin to feel mentally battered and accomplish little.

"The battered mind" describes a condition experienced by managers in business, industry, and government. These individuals spend their days running from one activity to another, never taking any time to think or to plan. Mentally and physically exhausted each evening, they return home unable to enjoy time with family and friends. Gradually, their energy is depleted and burnout sets in. Coaches often recognize the symptoms of the battered mind but unfortunately are convinced they must live with this state of mind until exhaustion forces them to resign. The mind is not equipped for that kind of consistent beating: The result is a dangerous form of helplessness which can easily affect others in the working environment. Coaches who have a battered mind are often the instigators of ACORN environments.

Coaches who realize that their minds are being battered admit to having some of these problems. Because they do not prioritize their work, they task hop, allow their minds to wander and digress, anticipate interruptions, and bounce up and down instead of attending to essential tasks. Rather than giving sustained attention to the truly important work, these coaches make constant interruption a tradition. Coaches will frequently swear that they do their best work under pressure. For some coaches, it seems that an approaching deadline is the only way to motivate interest and stimulate real effort.

Coaches who admit to the battered mind note the rapid pace of life and the insufficient time they have to accomplish all their responsibilities. These coaches, who should be in control of the environment, are slaves to a multitude of external forces they believe are beyond their control. Instead of closing office doors or asking people to come back later, they come in early, give up lunch, stay late, and work on weekends—and still, there is more to do!

ANALYZE YOURSELF

In the last chapter Sarah Stiel, Frank Adams, and others in the athletic program suffered a number of unpleasant experiences because of poor time management. These poor time managers created ACORN environments in which people moved from crisis to crisis. The coaches became tense and exhausted; they accomplished less and even this was done poorly.

Five management problems were identified which contributed to the development of an ACORN environment—a situation in which people become Aggressive, Compulsive, Ornery, and Really Nutty. As you read the chapter you probably began wondering about the effectiveness of your own time management skills. You may already be aware of some problem areas, but it is difficult to evaluate yourself objectively. To help you evaluate your ACORN tendencies, you should respond honestly to the questions listed in the ACORN—Self-Evaluation questionnaire.

ACORN—SELF-EVALUATION

Use this questionnaire to assess your ACORN-creating potential. All of us are prone to create environments similar to those of Sarah and Frank. By checking these questions once or twice a week, we can monitor our behavior and improve our time management. Circle the number which most accurately represents your honest response to the statement.

1. I rely on mythical time, putting off major work until "later."

1	2	3	4	5
Rarely		Sometimes		Often

2. I overestimate the amount of time I control each day.

1	2	3	4	5
Rarely		Sometimes		Often

3. I readily accept new tasks and am reluctant to say no to a request.

1	2	3	4	5
Rarely		Sometimes		Often

4. My days are spent hopping from one task to another because concentrating is difficult where I work.

1	2	3	4	5
Rarely		Sometimes		Often

5. My door regularly stays open as an invitation to drop-in visitors.

1	2	3	4	5
Rarely		Sometimes		Often

6. I will put aside my work if a colleague requests assistance.

1	2	3	4	5
Rarely		Sometimes		Often

7. I frequently change priorties if a new task or idea interests me.

1	2	3	4	5
Rarely		Sometimes		Often

8. My best work is done under deadline pressure and I usually finish just in time.

1	2	3	4	5
Rarely		Sometimes		Often

9. I am sensitive to others' need for privacy to accomplish their work.

1	2	3	4	5
Rarely		Sometimes		Often

10. Those with whom I work feel pressured because of my tendencies to procrastinate.

1	2	3	4	5
Rarely		Sometimes		Often

What was your score? If your total was 40 or above, beware of ACORN-related problems. A total between 30 and 40 is cause for concern. Regardless of where you scored, avoid complacency. Even the best time managers can slip. It is a good idea to check your answers with colleagues, for you may discover they perceive your behavior differently.

This simple, self-evaluation may have revealed time management problems you had not previously noticed. Unfortunately, the self-evaluation does suffer from the limitation that it relies on your perceptions of reality. It is possible you failed to observe other problems that exist. To help you identify specific problems, a useful technique is to self-monitor.

SELF-MONITORING

Self-monitoring involves collecting detailed data on what happens each day. Many consultants on executive effectiveness suggest that time be recorded in 15- or 30-minute intervals. An alternative and less time-consuming monitoring technique is to set aside two 10-minute periods, one prior to noon, the other before leaving in the afternoon, to review what you have done that day. Shown below is the format for a time chart on which you can record your daily activities.

Date: _____   Name: _____
Time   **Activity**
6:00 am
6:30
7:00
7:30
8:00
8:30
9:00
9:30
10:00
10:30
11:00
11:30
12:00
12:30 pm
1:00
1:30
2:00
2:30

Date: _____   Name: _____
Time   **Activity**
3:00
3:30
4:00
4:30
5:00
5:30
6:00
6:30
7:00
7:30
8:00
8:30
9:00
9:30
10:00
10:30
11:00
11:30

By self-monitoring, data replace conjecture. Our memories are so fragile that it is easy to forget what we plan to do, as well as what we have done. With periodic self-monitoring, you can take snapshots of your busy life. The time chart on page 25 can be used to analyze specific days that may be more important than others: for example, the days leading up to a major game or competition, the period immediately after it, or the time spent on a recruiting trip. The data you gather will make it easier to pinpoint ACORN-producing activities.

In private organizations, senior managers will often ask talented but disorganized employees to monitor their daily activities. After a week, these employees are generally shocked by what they observe. They become alert to where task creep begins and how easily a new option or interruption can throw them off track. These individuals continue by reviewing typical days at least three times a month. This enables them to pick up any backsliding and helps them catch the reappearance of bad habits. Many people elect to self-monitor more often, sometimes on specific days or for short periods on especially hectic days. The habit of self-monitoring is a way of keeping unproductive time-use practices from reappearing.

By completing the daily time chart, you will be taking an essential first step in time management. You must first know how you spend your time before you can plan how to use it more effectively. "But isn't keeping this log just an additional waste of time?" is a frequent question to the idea of a time chart. My response is to suggest they at least try the exercise, then evaluate its worth. Research has shown that most people are very inaccurate in assessing the time they spend on daily activities. For many, it is a revelation to discover they spend 2-3 hours a day on the phone or only 15 minutes a day on priority tasks. You will be able to determine objective standards by which to evaluate the effectiveness of your daily organization only after you know where your time goes.

Monitoring would be a valuable exercise to recommend to coaches like Sarah and Frank. The evidence of real data can lead to genuine improvement. To illustrate, we will examine how Sarah Stiel might have completed the time chart on the day we observed her behavior.

Date: MAY 8th Name: SARAH STIEL		Date: MAY 8th Name: SARAH STIEL
Time **Activity**		**Time** **Activity**
6:00 am WOKE, SHOWERED / DRESSED		3:00 FRANK VISITED (15 MIN.) / WALKED TO PRACTICE
6:30 BREAKFAST / DROVE TO UNIV		3:30 PRACTICE - DIDN'T GO WELL / ASSIST. COACHES WERE POORLY ORGANIZED
7:00 ARRIVED AT OFFICE / READ NEWSPAPER		4:00
7:30 CHECKED YESTERDAY'S MAIL		4:30 PRACTICE
8:00 CHATTED W/ SECRETARY & TRACK COACH		5:00
8:30 TRAINER CALLED - WON'T BE IN TODAY / ARRANGED SUB. TRAINER		5:30 PRACTICE FINISHED / SHOWERED, DROVE HOME
9:00 WORKED ON PRACTICE PLAN (10 MIN.) / TWO ATHLETES VISIT		6:00 SHOPPED FOR GROCERIES
9:30 DISCUSSED W/BILL & WENDY - APPOINT. OF NEW DEPT. STAFF / COFFEE IN COACHES ROOM		6:30 ARRIVED HOME / FIXED MEAL
10:00 DISCUSSED INVENT. REPORT W/JOAN - OFFERED TO HELP / SUE CALLED - I'LL GET STATE CONF. SPEAKERS		7:00 DID DISHES / BEGAN LAUNDRY
10:30 LOOKED FOR MEET REG. FORMS & PLAYER APPLICATIONS / A.D. CALLED - MUST COMPLETE UNITED WAY COLLECTIONS		7:30 LAUNDRY
11:00 BEGAN LETTERS TO RECRUITS (10 MIN.) / BEGAN PREPARING SPEECH FOR BOOSTER CLUB (15 MIN.)		8:00 WORKED ON MEET REG - LEFT FILE AT WORK (10 MIN.) / PEG CALLED, DISCUSSED CA. VISIT
11:30 LEFT REG. FOR SECRETARY TO FINISH / DROVE TO LUNCHEON		8:30 DRAFTED RECRUITING LETTERS (15 MIN.)
12:00 LUNCH		9:00 READ SPORTS JOURNAL
12:30 pm SPOKE TO BOOSTERS		9:30 WROTE TO PARENTS / TOM CALLED (15 MIN.)
1:00 MET ATHLETES ON CAMPUS		10:00 WATCHED TV WHILE FOLDING CLOTHES / LEZLI CALLED - CAN'T PLAY THIS WEEKEND
1:30 BEGAN PLANNING PRACTICE (10 MIN.) / JW VISITED (PERSONAL PROBLEM)		10:30 WATCHED REST OF TV SHOW
2:00 SECRETARY RETURNED MEET REG. - NEW INFO NEEDED / JW STAYED 'TIL 2:30		11:00 GOT READY FOR BED / SLEPT
2:30 BEGAN FILLING IN MEET REG. (8 MIN.) / STARTED LETTERS TO RECRUITS (7 MIN.)		11:30

If Sarah looked at the chart carefully, she would begin to notice how her day was filled with constant interruptions and how little time she actually spent working toward her goals.

A clearer analysis of this data can be seen if we divide it under headings representing the major activities in Sarah's daily schedule. Table 2.1 illustrates this next step.

Table 2.1
Time Chart Analysis

Activities	Hours
Personal	
Sleep 11 p.m.—6 a.m.	7
Shower, dress	½
Breakfast	¼
Lunch	1
Dinner	½
Laundry	1
Store	½
	10¾
Travel	
To office	¼
To and from luncheon	¼
To and from practice	½
Home	¼
	1¼
Work-Coaching	
Routine calls/mail	1½
Secretary (10+10+10)	½
Meetings (unplanned)	1½
(planned)	½
Interruptions (by others)	2
(self-imposed)	1
Planning for priority tasks	1
Conducting priority tasks (practice)	2
Changing	¼
	10¼
Leisure	
Read newspapers	½
Read sports journal	¼
TV	½
Talk to Tom	¼
	1½
Family	
Write a letter (not finished)	¼
	¼

The Time Chart Analysis clearly shows how inefficiently Sarah used her time on this particular day. She (a) spent only 60 minutes of the entire day planning priority tasks, (b) spent 90 minutes in unplanned meetings, (c) was continually interrupted throughout the day for a total of 2 hours, and (d) wasted 1 hour of her time on self-imposed interruptions.

From this analysis it is easier to see how much time Sarah wastes each day on nonessential tasks, and how little time she devotes to her major responsibilities. Looking at these figures might help Sarah understand why she never seems able to catch up or finish her assignments. However, analyzing only one day might give a distorted impression of her time use. Sarah ought to keep a Time Chart for a week. Everyone occasionally experiences exceptional days of unexpected distractions resulting in lost time. Over a week the exceptions become less noticable, and a regular pattern of time-use emerges. The following are some of the insights Sarah would gain:

- An average of 2 hours a day is spent in conversation.
- Only 10-15 minutes a day is spent planning for practice.
- Interruptions are a continual problem.
- Poor organization of paperwork causes much waste of time.

Through self-monitoring, time management problems become more apparent. Until coaches understand they are experiencing management problems, it is futile to suggest possible remedies. If coaches like Sarah and Frank can be encouraged to monitor themselves, they will begin to recognize the need for improvement. They may also begin to appreciate the stressful environments they create for colleagues, as well as the limitations their behavior places on the success of the overall athletic program. Many of the problems the two coaches faced were discussed in detail in chapter 1. To resolve these organizational problems, the best approach is to try to improve your time management skills rather than dwell on the negative. This will help prevent the emergence of the original difficulties. Sarah and Frank would benefit from this approach, and it will also work for you.

Before continuing to learn about techniques for improving your management of time, it is essential to become aware of your existing behavior. You need to collect objective data and analyze how effectively you currently manage time. Even if you feel you are already an effective time manager, you will benefit most from this book by conducting an objective examination. Use the time charts previously presented, and through careful analysis, try to identify a few areas in which you feel there is some room for improvement.

Once you understand the pattern of your own time use, the next step toward becoming a good time manager is to identify the techniques you already use to manage time. At the end of each day for a 1- to 2-week period, spend 5 to 10 minutes reviewing your accomplishments. Try to identify which organizing techniques you regularly or periodically use. For example, do you have a daily schedule? Do you set aside periods of time to complete assignments? Do you have a system for dealing with routine paperwork? Some of you may discover you already have a system which works. If so, reading this book will reinforce your experiences and boost your self-confidence. Additional techniques to improve your time management will be suggested throughout this book. These will reduce your ACORN-causing tendencies and will increase your productivity. For the moment, however, let us begin by emphasizing what already works and build on existing foundations. List on two reminder cards the useful techniques you already use.

To remind yourself of the techniques you now use, leave one card in your coaches' room or office and another at home. Put the cards in visible locations—for example, above your telephone or on your clipboard. You may also want to carry a copy with you as a constant reference whenever you feel a need for direction. This is the reverse of the "out of sight, out of mind" principle; it increases the probability you will use the techniques you have chosen.

For the first week or two, review these lists at the end of each day. What did you achieve? Focus on your successes—for example, a well-planned practice, a routine assignment completed, or a major competition arranged. Carefully evaluate the extent to which your existing time management techniques contributed to these successes. The steps for constructing your own personal method for successful time management are listed below.

- Write down techniques which already work on reminder index cards.
- Post them in visible locations.
- Review them as a habitual part of your daily routine.
- Relate accomplishments to the regular use of your techniques.

As you continue reading this book, keep some index cards nearby and note down any ideas that appeal to you. It is unrealistic to expect to become an effective time manager overnight. This ability is developed slowly by experimenting with a variety of organizing methods and by discovering what works best for you. Your goal is to construct a *personal recipe* for successful time mangement. We will return to this list and its use in the introduction to Part 2 and again in chapter 10. By then, you will have had the chance to modify or adapt your ideas based on the advice given in the following chapters.

SUMMARY AND RECOM-MENDATIONS

To become effective time managers, coaches must first understand the extent to which the success of their programs is *dependent* on *their* organizational skills. Listed below are considerations to make when analyzing your ability to manage time:

1. If you attempt too much or fail to control the pressures in your environment, you will not realize your coaching potential and will frustrate the efforts of others in the athletic program.

2. Remain alert to behaviors which create ACORN environments.

3. Self-evaluation and self-monitoring are two methods for identifying time management problems.

4. Analyzing the data collected on a daily time chart provides objective evidence of your effectiveness as a time manager.

5. Recognizing areas where there is room for improving your time use will give you the motivation to attempt remedial action.

6. List the organizing techniques you already use on reminder cards, and relate your accomplishments to the effectiveness of these techniques.

Once you understand the effectiveness of your own time management skills, you can begin to consider methods for improvement. You must build on the basis of your existing organizational skills. The next chapter will examine the necessity of establishing a clear direction as you organize your program.

Chapter 3
Establishing Direction

1
Time Management and Sports
a. Ineffective time management
b. The ACORN environment

2
Analyzing Time Use
a. Self-evaluation and self-monitoring
b. Personal time management recipes

3
Establishing Direction
a. Setting goals, priorities, and limits
b. Detail management

4
Maintaining Control
a. Active concentration
b. Stress—and distress management

5-9
Time Management Techniques in Practice

Goal Setting (Chap. 5)
Routine Planning (Chap. 6)
Task Orienting (Chap. 7)
Demand Control (Chap. 8)
Limit Maintenance (Chap. 9)

10
Starting and Maintaining Effective Time Management
a. Selecting and using techniques
b. Reaching out to others

GOAL SETTING

Good time management is not an end in itself but rather a means to an end. It can make you personally more efficient and create a pleasant and productive working environment for your staff. But to be successful, you must clearly identify the ends you are seeking. You need direction. The first step in developing effective time management skills is to clearly define your goals. Goals give you a basis for setting priorities, making decisions, and working for some things while eliminating others. Realistic goals and a sense of direction will prevent the creation of an ACORN environment.

"Which path shall I take?" Alice asked the March Hare when she came to a crossroad. "Where do you want to go?" the Hare responded. "I don't know!" Alice admitted. "Then the choice isn't important" replied the Hare.

The Hare's message is clear and valid: Proceeding without a sense of direction and specific goals is often a waste of time and energy. Goals provide the foundation for a successful athletic program. Many kinds of goals can be set: lifetime, 5-year, 1-year, seasonal. The choice is yours, but it is essential you identify a clear sense of immediate direction.

Your goals will depend on your coaching philosophy. The philosophy endorsed by the American Coaching Effectiveness Program is *Athletes First, Winning Second*. This philosophy emphasizes that your first goal is to help all your athletes fully develop their physical, emotional, mental, and social abilities. Athletes who understand you are primarily concerned with their development and their striving for success will enjoy participating in your program regardless of game results. Removing the fear of failure helps athletes to perform better and, in the long term, achieve greater success.

It is *unrealistic* to evaluate the success of your athletic program solely on the basis of your win-loss record. In sport, not every team can win, and many factors other than individual or team performance contribute to the final game result. It is important to instill in your athletes the understanding that winning or losing should not be the measure of their success. In trying to plan a successful, beneficial, and enjoyable athletic program, you must first be *realistic*.

Setting Realistic Goals

Ideally, before the season begins, you should identify realistic goals. These must include your coaching goals and quality of life goals which include activities with family and friends and time for relaxation, hobbies, self-improvement, and perhaps some community obligations. Success-driven coaches easily forget these essential activities. If you fail to set limits on what you will attempt, you will eliminate personal time for activites other than coaching. Sarah is an example of this type of coach. Because of her willingness to try to do everything, she failed to complete anything successfully. For a busy coach, a more effective approach is to do less better *and* to find time to stop.

"I don't have time to relax, let alone develop a hobby," busy and often overcommitted individuals will exclaim. These individuals describe all their responsibilities, their committees, meetings, reports, special projects, and extra assignments. Because they could not say no, they created a packed schedule with no time left for rest and fun. These individuals soon wear out and, in the long run, will never feel successful.

A realistic blend of professional and personal goals should be the motivation for managing time. You must clearly identify your goals and share them with colleagues, athletes, and family members. Write your program goals and give everyone associated with the program a copy. This sense of direction will help you stay in control of your day. Without control, it is difficult and often impossible to accomplish any goals.

The Process of Establishing General Goals

To give you some idea of this goal-setting process, you should begin by choosing general goals for your career (which may or may not be full-time coaching), family, personal development, and community service. For example Sarah Stiel might establish the following general goals:

Coaching Goal

To be an effective university coach and to help all my athletes fully develop their physical, emotional, mental, and social abilities.

Family

To live in a midsized community near the ocean, earning a salary which will enable me to buy my own home. To marry and raise a small family.

Personal Development

To keep fit, to learn how to prepare vegetarian meals, to improve my guitar playing, and to learn French so I can visit Paris during the vacation.

Community Service

To continue offering coaching clinics for young athletes during the summer vacation, and to actively support other community events (but to avoid overcommitting myself).

General goals tend to be vague statements of future directions you would like to follow. They provide a basis for identifying more specific goals which will lead to the adoption of certain patterns of behavior. For example, Sarah's general coaching goal demands attention to the creation of a well-organized athletic program. Before Sarah can begin planning the steps necessary to achieve this goal, she must decide whether the goal is one of her priorities. By selecting this goal, she may have to postpone, temporarily or permanently, the realization of other general goals.

SETTING PRIORITIES

It is not realistic to set, or to expect to achieve goals without first deciding priorities. Your priorities are your street signs; without them, you can wander down any number of side streets and never reach your destination.

To change metaphors, imagine your priorities as a set of three concentric circles. The inner ring in this picture contains the work that only you can do—These are your highest priority tasks. As events occur, ask yourself if they fit into this inner ring. Remember, that some routine chores have priority; for example, the registration forms that Sarah and Frank neglected to fill out were in this ring.

The maintenance of your program is a high priority. Shown below is a list of highest priority tasks gleaned from conversations with successful coaches. As your program grows and matures, you can add new challenges or variations to this inner ring. But, as several coaches have advised, "Do the tricky stuff once the basics are in place!"

Program Maintenance Activities
- Planning practices
- Monitoring individual and team performances
- Planning for competitions
- Necessary paperwork
- Time for athletes to discuss problems

Program Building Activities
- Providing information to leadership
- General public relations
- Recruiting
- Program monitoring
- Facilities and equipment review

In addition to the tasks you have labelled "highest priority," you may want to consider a second ring of "maybe" tasks. You may get to one of these assignments or activities, if there is time, but only after the highest priority tasks are finished or under control. Remember, Murphy's Law states that everything takes longer than expected. Do not be like Sarah who trapped herself in the low-priority tasks of the second and third ring groups of activities.

This third ring contains "never do" activities. These might include agreeing to referee a game, volunteering to help another coach, or taking on more committee assignments. Although they may be pleasant and even helpful services, avoid these tasks, for tasks in the third ring take precious time away from those essential tasks in the inner ring.

Coaching, either on a full-time or part-time basis, is a time-consuming job. It is easy for busy and committed coaches to forget the time they need for themselves and for loved ones. This personal time also belongs in the inner ring. Just like a savings account, you must set aside a little time each day, or you may find too late that you have nothing at all. For example, from her list of general goals, Sarah Stiel ought to identify activities other than those related to coaching for inclusion in her list of high priorities. She might include some of the following:

- Taking a daily midday break to run or exercise
- Attending a guitar class two evenings a week
- Leaving work no later than 6 p.m. every day and becoming more socially active
- Visiting her parents at least once a week

Another coach might include the following list of personal activities in this inner ring of high priorities:

- Withdrawing to think, to plan, and to organize in anticipation of major events
- Relaxing by reading a book, fishing, running, napping, or watching a television show
- Being with family or friends
- Enjoying a hobby or pastime that removes my mind from coaching

You must identify activities which are meaningful to you and so develop your own personal recipe for successful time management. If you are intent on achieving success as a coach, one of your priorities must be to set and to achieve realistic seasonal goals. Let us examine some of the key elements this task involves.

Season Plan

One of your most important coaching tasks is to develop a season plan, which includes everything you wish to teach in the upcoming season: for example, sport skills, rules, sportsmanship, and strategies. The process of developing this plan was outlined in detail in the ACEP Level 1 text *Coaching Young Athletes* (Martens, Christina, Harvey, & Sharkey, 1981). The first step in preparing this plan is to establish your instructional goals. These goals need to be compatible with your coaching philosophy and the philosophy of your sport organization.

Shown in Table 3.1 are two sets of realistic instructional goals: The first set is for a novice wrestling team of 10- to 13-year-olds, and the second for an advanced soccer team of 13- to 15-year-olds.

Instructional goals are general statements of what you hope your athletes will know or be able to do at the end of the season. Notice that the goals include much more than just techniques. Consideration is made of all areas contributing

Table 3.1
Examples of Instructional Goals for Two Sports

Novice Wrestling (Ages 10-13)	Advanced Soccer (Ages 13-15)
The wrestlers will be able to demonstrate: 1. Mastery of the fundamental wrestling skills necessary to successfully participate in practices and matches at a novice level. 2. Knowledge of proper nutritional and safe weight control practices and ability to apply it to themselves. 3. Accurate and complete knowledge of basic rules of the sport. 4. Appropriate sportsmanship behaviors in practices and games. 5. Knowledge and application of the basic strategies needed to effectively participate in matches at the novice level.	The soccer players will be able to demonstrate: 1. Mastery of advanced individual soccer skills necessary to participate in games at this level. 2. Acquisition of the offensive and defensive patterns of team play needed to successfully participate in games at this level. 3. Appropriate sportsmanship behaviors in practices and games. 4. Development of positive personal qualities in practices and games.

to the development of a complete athlete. Winning is not included as a goal because it is unrealistic to predict individual or team results with any accuracy.

Using these goals for direction, coaches can organize plans for achievement. This involves the selection of skills as shown in Table 3.2, and the organization of an instructional schedule as in Table 3.3.

Once the instruction of skills has been organized, the coach can develop a series of more specific sub-goals of expected knowledge or behavior for each of the remaining instructional goals. For example, the wrestling coach who wanted his athletes to demonstrate "appropriate sportsmanship behaviors in practices and matches" might develop the list of specific behaviors shown in Table 3.4.

The weekly practice schedule should be based on the organization of skill instruction. Other specific behaviors the coach wishes to emphasize, for example, sportsmanship behaviors—should be listed and referred to when planning for practice. Regularly reviewing these lists will enable coaches to select appropriate behaviors (rules or knowledge) to emphasize during practice sessions.

Table 3.2
Individual Skills Selected to Achieve Wrestling Goal 1

Goal 1
The wrestlers will be able to demonstrate they have mastered the fundamental wrestling skills necessary to successfully participate in practices and matches at a novice level.

Individual Skills

Takedowns
1. Do's and Don'ts
2. Tie Ups
3. Double Leg
4. Single Leg
5. Arm Drag
6. Fireman's Carry
7. Duck Under

Counters to Takedowns
1. Defense on Your Feet
2. Hip Block
3. Whizzer
4. Cross Face
5. ¼ Nelson
6. Pancake

Escapes and Reversals
1. Referee's Starting Position
2. Do's and Don'ts
3. Stand Up
4. Sit Back, Turn In
5. Hip Roll
6. Switch

Counters to Escapes and Reversals
1. Counter to Stand Up
2. Counter to Sit Back, Turn In
3. Counter to Hip Roll
4. Counter to Switch

Breakdowns and Rides
1. Do's and Don'ts
2. Cross Face-Near Leg
3. Far Ankle-Knee Bump
4. Far Ankle-Waist
5. Two on One Ride

Counters to Breakdowns and Rides
1. Counter to Cross Face-Near Leg
2. Counter to Ankle-Knee Bump
3. Counter to Far Ankle-Waist
4. Counter to Two on One Ride

Pinning Combinations
1. Half Nelson
2. Cross Face Cradle
3. Arm Bar-Reverse Half
4. ¾ Nelson

Counters to Pinning Combinations
1. Regaining a Base
2. Counter to Half Nelson
3. Counter to Arm Bar
5. Counter to ¾ Nelson

Table 3.3
Partial Instructional Schedule for Wrestling Goal 1

Goal 1: The wrestlers will be able to demonstrate they have mastered the fundamental wrestling skills necessary to successfully participate in practices and matches at a novice level

Skills	Month 1 Week 1 T	Week 1 TH	Week 2 T	Week 2 TH	Week 3 T	Week 3 TH	Week 4 T	Week 4 TH	Month 2 Week 1 T	Week 1 TH	Week 2 T	Week 2 TH	...etc ...etc ...etc	Time (in minutes) Spent on Each Skill for the Season
Takedowns														
1. Do's & Don'ts	T(10)	P(10)	P(5)						P(5)					30
2. Tie Ups	T(15)	P(10)	P(10)	P(10)					P(10)					55
3. Double Leg			T(15)	P(15)	P(10)	P(10)					P(10)	P(10)		70
4. Single Leg					T(15)	P(15)	P(10)	P(10)				P(10)		60
													Total Time	215
Counters to Takedowns														
1. Defense on Feet	T(15)	P(10)	P(5)				P(10)							40
2. Hip Block							T(15)	P(10)	P(10)					35
3. Whizzer								T(10)	P(10)					20
4. Cross Face									T(10)	P(10)				20
													Total Time	115
Escapes & Reversals														
1. Referee's Starting Position	T(10)	P(5)												15
2. Do's & Don'ts	T(10)	P(5)	P(10)						P(5)					25
3. Stand Up			T(10)	P(15)	P(10)	P(10)	P(10)	P(10)						65
4. Switch					T(15)	P(15)	P(10)	P(10)						50
													Total Time	155
. . . etc													. . . . etc	

Note:
T(10) = Teach skill for the first time in 10 minutes
P(10) = Practice or drill the skill as a team for 10 minutes
As the season progresses, individual practice time should be built into your instructional schedule so that your athletes can practice what they would like.

Table 3.4
Sportsmanship Behaviors Selected to Achieve Wrestling Goal 4

> **Goal 4**
> The wrestlers will be able to demonstrate appropriate sportsmanship behaviors in practices and matches.

Sportsmanship Behaviors

1. Demonstrates proper control of emotions.
2. Demonstrates use of appropriate language.
3. Is courteous to opponents, teammates, officials, coaches, and parents.
4. Is humble in winning and gracious in defeat.
5. Respects opponent as a person in winning and losing.
6. Abides by the rules of wrestling and never intentionally uses questionable holds or attempts to punish an opponent.

Performance Goals

The goals you establish in your season plan must relate specifically to performance and not to results. Remember, you and your athletes have control only over performance goals, *not* over the game result. Coaches should never establish seasonal goals such as "winning the championship" or "getting to state finals." These are unrealistic and almost certain to fail. You and your athletes will inevitably be disappointed, even though in many respects your season may have been tremendously successful.

Performance goals enable coaches and athletes to see genuine improvements. Improvement is a sign of success and should be rewarded. Athletes who fail to win competitions and yet improve their performances can feel proud of themselves, for they are successful. Perhaps you have already noticed how outstanding athletes who fail to win Olympic medals or major competitions are sometimes labeled as failures. It is unfair to impose these unrealistic goals on athletes. Clearly, just to be selected for an Olympic team is a major success and deserves praise, not criticism. Coaches should help athletes of all ages and abilities to set and to achieve realistic performance goals. These goals will enhance motivation and maintain enthusiasm throughout the season.

Sharing Goals

How coaches manage environments, not just individuals was described in chapter 1. Does your organization support *your* goals and share *your* direction and expectations? It is unwise to assume that you understand the expectations of your athletic director, school president, or club president. Similarly, do not assume that they understand your expectations.

Arrange to meet with the heads of your organization to find out what they expect from their athletic program and from their coaches. Be sure to have a well-thought-out plan with you; it can be the best spokesman you have. Show them your plans, delineate your philosophy, and discuss any organizational changes you wish to make. It is much easier to build and to maintain a program when you know exactly what you can and cannot do, and when you know that you will have support whether or not you keep the trophy cases filled.

Successful coaches build realistic programs slowly and carefully. They determine what progress will be possible over one or more seasons given the level of available support and talent. At this stage, they determine responsibilities and delegate tasks accordingly. These coaches then establish milestones for evaluating individual and team progress at different points throughout the season.

DETAIL MANAGEMENT

Coaching is full of details regardless of the level of competition or the age of the participants. If you forget or neglect these details you may prevent progress or even ruin an athletic program. To have time to coach, you must first learn to manage all the details that go with coaching. Some details only you can handle. *Delegate* the less important details to others, and *eliminate* the details that are unimportant, unrelated, and unrealistic.

Seasonal Details

To reach your goals, you must take the time to plan, and planning involves careful thought and foresight. Detail management demands the same kind of close attention. What are details? They are the tiny aspects of organization so easy to overlook yet which can significantly affect the success of your athletic program. For example, have you ever arrived at a locked sport facility that you expected to find open? Or perhaps your team finished a game in the middle of winter and you discovered that the showers were cold because no one had remembered to turn on the water heater. These "minor" details can assume enormous proportions if you are not prepared.

Preseason Planning

A high school athletic director and basketball coach of 17 years recently told me, "I write the details down before the season begins. Two other people then check the list to make sure nothing has been forgotten." A number of other program heads reported taking the same comprehensive first steps in detail management. One parent in charge of a county-wide swimming team for elementary and middle school-age children kept a notebook containing specifics on how long trips to distant towns took, the amount of spending money swimmers should bring along, and how many officials were needed at a meet. Similar records were kept by the coach of a Little League baseball team. In a four-page handout, he told parents when practices would be held, what players should wear to games, which parents should bring drinks, and when rides were needed for away games. These coaches have discovered that once the details of a season are in place, it is much easier to assign specific responsibilities.

Before the season begins, you should meet with your assistant coaches, your athletes, and their parents to discuss organization for the upcoming season. This is the time to discuss your coaching philosophy and expectations. A Parent Orientation Program is an ideal way of communicating to parents and athletes how you intend to organize your program. Misunderstandings between parents and coaches are a frequent cause of conflict. (See chapter 18 of *Coaching Young Athletes* for information about how to plan a Parent Orientation Program). To remind you of many of the preseason details which need consideration, a sample preseason planning checklist is shown.

PRESEASON PLANNING CHECKLIST

_____ Know the structure and operation of your youth sports organization.

_____ Establish your philosophy and style of coaching.

_____ Prepare an instructional outline and schedule for the season.

_____ Plan registration.

_____ Arrange transportation for the athletes.

_____ Plan for the selection of a team captain.

_____ Establish team rules and penalties with your team.

_____ Plan a Parent Orientation Program.

_____ Prepare and obtain instructional aids and materials.

_____ Schedule days and times of practices and games.

_____ Schedule facilities for practices and games.

_____ Schedule officials for games.

_____ Arrange for the preparation of the playing area for practice sessions and games.

_____ Establish inclement weather practice procedures for outdoor sports.

_____ Arrange for protection of valuables during practice.

_____ Select assistant coaches and plan the season with them.

_____ Plan for a postseason evaluation of your program.

_____ Arrange for your athletes to have medical examinations.

_____ Plan a conditioning program.

_____ Know how accident expenses are covered.

_____ Know what to do in case of an accident.

_____ Plan proper safety procedures.

_____ Obtain personal liability insurance if you are not protected.

Delegating Responsibilities

The players on one soccer team always had halftime drinks and cut-up oranges because their coach asked each player's parents to be responsible for drinks and oranges at one game. He also organized a telephone notification system which kept all players informed of changes; no parent had to make more than two telephone calls using his system. This volunteer coach was regional sales manager for a large national oil company. "Effective managers get work done with the help of others," he commented. By assigning a few details to parents, he was able to concentrate on organizing practices and coaching the soccer players.

Of course, some coaches do not have parents willing to help, much less assistants, managers, or secretaries. The entire program is theirs to manage. "You do what you can and don't let the details overwhelm what must be done to produce a successful program," a volunteer swimming coach said. "Some records of individual performance just won't be kept," he went on to explain. "When your primary emphasis is on developing swimmers, the 'must' details are very clear. I tell my swimmers they are responsible for warm-up, equipment, and for keeping individual time records. My job is limited to planning and running practices and preparing for meets."

If you coach on your own, staying within the inner ring of highest priority tasks is critical. Certain details such as arrangements for travel to a game, required registration forms, and player medical records must be taken care of. These are the details absolutely necessary for program operation. The rest you must put aside. Concentrate solely on your highest priorities.

Competition Details

Before a game or competition, there are always special details that need attention: The location may be new; different shoes, clothing, or other equipment may be needed; the players may be introduced in a different way. These small matters can escalate if they are not given attention.

Competition should be given a little extra attention and difficulties or complications foreseen. "I call it problem anticipation," one wrestling coach reported. "Each meet can produce special situations and associated problems, which by looking ahead, can be identified, anticipated, and eliminated."

The time you devote to special preparation will vary depending upon the sport, the setting, and the age of participants. Does the team know when and where the game is to be played? What color jerseys will they wear? Who will bring the equipment, and how will it get there? Although the details become more complex as the level of the sport increases, foreseeing details is crucial for all coaches. By taking care of the minor details before competition, you free yourself to concentrate solely on the game itself.

Sometimes these minor details, if unattended, can have serious consequences. For example, an assistant sprint coach on the 1972 U.S. Olympic Track and Field Team was responsible for ensuring that two sprinters made it to their qualifying heats. However, the coach believed the athletes had to be at the stadium at a later time than originally set. He did not bother to recheck such a crucial detail the day before the heats; as a result, the athletes arrived late and, after years of training, missed the opportunity to compete.

Eliminating Details From Practice

While managing important details will help you organize the season, *eliminating* unnecessary details can also improve the organization and discipline of your practice sessions. Establishing a *routine* is crucial when planning practices. Practices which follow a regular, well-known routine, especially in the period immediately preceeding competition, are easier to administer and usually more successful. "My team knows when the season starts what practice plan will be followed," a ski coach reported. "There is room for flexibility and change, but the basic routine remains the same."

Agreeing with that approach, a high school track coach added that routine lets athletes know what will be expected of them each day. "They have certain drills to do, required conditioning and performance improvement targets to reach. I can't be all over the track supervising. This organization allows me to concentrate attention on a few athletes and to know the rest are working." By creating a routine, you leave yourself time for spotting and eliminating problems, observing drills, and helping individual athletes.

SETTING LIMITS

The graphic example of priority-setting shown on page 36 is your reminder to set limits. You must decide where each new activity belongs. Is it a first-, second-, or third-priority activity? These decisions will not always be clear-cut, and sometimes you must take a chance. But the potential for task creep is enormous; avoiding Sarah's environment of panic and chaos is your best reason for setting limits.

Although establishing limits is theoretically simple, in practice you may initially find it difficult. Setting appropriate limits takes planning, and planning requires careful thought. It is easy to maintain old procedures simply from habit. Habit prevents us from questioning how we operate, even if we are operating poorly. Instead of taking the time to see if we have taken on too much or are overaccessible, we simply assume that we are operating as best we can. The result is a lack of improvement, efficiency, or change.

The best way to set limits is to say no. Although Sarah and Frank operate very differently, they are alike in their unwillingness to regularly say no. Sarah will not turn down unimportant tasks, and Frank will not stop procrastinating. Contrast their approach with the following comments from several time conscientious coaches:

- "I won't take on speaking engagements at all during the season."
- "Recruiting is the only other major activity for the season besides practices. I make time before and after games to watch prospects."
- "The responsibilities of assistant coaches are discussed and assigned well before the season begins. Each has specific duties which I know will be handled well."
- "My family knows they will see me less during the season. They aren't forgotten but preparation requires more time away from home. We talk about this sacrifice and they understand."
- "I find time to get away from the pressure to think, even relax during the season—an absolute necessity two or three times a week."
- "I organize details before the season begins so that arrangements can be made early and most of the time by

other people. These are never forgotten but don't get in the way of my major responsibilities."

- "I am less available to media and set up certain times when interviews will be arranged. I make some exceptions for the national media and distant reporters."

A single message emerges from all of these comments: Time is a scarce resource; you must use it intelligently and concentrate on a few critical goal-oriented activities. Think about your own coaching program. What have you done to establish limits? Have you made clear to others what you will and will not be doing? Have you obtained their agreement to these limits? How effectively do you delegate tasks among your assistants? If your days are spent running, reacting, and agreeing to do more, setting limits could improve this situation. Use the following list of reminders for setting limits to seasonal tasks.

Reminders for Setting Limits

1. Allocate time to plan practices and do not allow that time to be eroded, except for obvious emergencies.

2. Determine what *you* must do, and which assignments can be delegated to assistants, athletes, parents, and others in your program.

3. Do not allow details to overwhelm you at the last minute: Organize and assign them before the season begins.

4. Focus attention and available time on helping young athletes to develop; consider saying no to activities not directly related to that priority task.

5. Set aside time to relax, to withdraw, and to evaluate the season.

EVALUATING YOUR PROGRAM

Coaches who are successful time managers find some time each week and often each day to look back and then ahead. They compare what has already been accomplished with the time and work remaining. These coaches review their athletes' progress, examine individual and team performance in practices and games, and consider any problems such as poor relationships among players and the team's general attitude. They check up on assignments and evaluate the performance of assistant coaches, managers, and other assistants. In the final step they identify any changes that need to be made—for example, shifting workloads or altering assignments. Although these coaches are not necessarily looking for trouble, they are trying to avoid the difficulties that often appear when one becomes too complacent or lost in details.

Evaluating involves taking a step back from each day's busy routine. "In my mind, I see the entire program and the current season as they come together," a college basketball coach reported. He asked himself if his program was on the right track and found that by removing himself some distance from it, he could come up with an intelligent and accurate answer.

"I find a few moments after practices to evaluate," one swimming coach commented. "That is a lull period after a very busy time. Before practice, there is too much to do to think clearly." Another coach reported taking an hour or two off just to walk and to evaluate the program and season. "That time is part relaxation and part planning," she said. "The more planning and evaluation I do, the more relaxed I am."

The size of your program will dictate how much monitoring and planning is required. Even if you are not a full-time coach, you should take some time to think through what you are doing. As several volunteer coaches have observed, "That is how we manage our professional lives. Why should coaching be any different?" Use the questions below to help evaluate the condition of your own program.

1. How are individual athletes and the total program progressing? Is the rate of progress compatible with preseason goals?

2. Are any problems beginning to appear? Between athletes? Between athletes and coaches?

3. Do *I* need to do more in certain areas or should I delegate more to others?

4. What is the general team mood now? Does it need any "perking up?"

DIRECTION BRINGS IMPROVEMENT

Let us consider how goals, plans, priorities, and other direction-setting techniques could improve Sarah Stiel's athletic program. Sarah would start each day knowing what had to be done and could prioritize her day's tasks. In spite of interruptions, Sarah would stay with one task to completion. If assistants, friends, or others asked for her help, she would be more likely to say no because of her sense of time and physical limitations. Her vulnerability to task creep would be reduced.

With her goal orientation supported by a plan, Sarah would be less likely to hop from task to task. She would become more willing to delegate responsibilities to others in the athletic program and be able to concentrate her attention on high-priority tasks. Also, she would take on less and would not feel so pressured by a constantly expanding workload. Then in the time she has available, she could further her program objectives. Sarah would be determined rather than compulsive. More importantly, Sarah would realize she can be in charge of her work and life and enjoy the satisfaction of her achievements. Her talents would be used to help athletes grow and improve. And as head coach, her attitude would be infectious, enabling assistants, athletes, and support staff to use their time intelligently, too.

If Frank Adams recognized the need for goals and a plan, he might also appreciate that achievements are more likely with consistent effort, rather than last-minute panic. Frank claims he does his best work under pressure and tries to avoid planning in advance. This contradicts an old and proven adage: "By failing to plan, you plan to fail." Research has shown that every hour spent in planning may save 3 hours in execution.

A better approach would be to use the full week rather than the last 2 days of the week to prepare his team for an upcoming competition. A clear plan helps to set a measured pace. Frank might become more sensitive to others, instead of interrupting everyone early in the week and then later blaming them for the results of his own procrastination. A more consistent workload might also give Frank time to listen when he needs to listen and keep him from intruding on others' privacy.

SUMMARY AND RECOMMENDATIONS

Good time management is a means to an end. To effectively manage time, you must be clear in your own mind what you are attempting to achieve. Setting goals, priorities, and limits will give you and your program a clear sense of direction which will increase the success of your program and prevent the creation of an ACORN environment. As you consider establishing direction for your program, keep the following recommendations in mind:

1. Goals should reflect the philosophy of *Athletes First, Winning Second*. Emphasize player development rather than game results.

2. Base your program on realistic goals; these should take into account reasonable expectations of what can and cannot be done.

3. Establish seasonal goals, then plan how to achieve them.

4. Assistant coaches, players, and parents should know and understand the goals and the plan for the season.

5. Use the plan to help set limits and to determine what you and your assistants will not undertake during the season.

6. Before the season begins, focus your attention on detail management. Try to plan ahead and anticipate any organizational details which, if left unattended, could cause problems.

7. Evaluate yourself and your program to ensure both are staying within the limits you have established.

Uncertainty or indecision about what you are trying to achieve is the hallmark of an ineffective time manager. Establishing direction should be your first planning priority. In the next chapter you will learn how to sustain your attention on program direction by controlling distractions present in the coaching environment.

Chapter 4
Maintaining Control

1
Time Management and Sports
a. Ineffective time management
b. The ACORN environment

2
Analyzing Time Use
a. Self-evaluation and self-monitoring
b. Personal time management recipes

10
Starting and Maintaining Effective Time Management
a. Selecting and using techniques
b. Reaching out to others

5-9
Time Management Techniques in Practice

Goal Setting (Chap. 5)
Routine Planning (Chap. 6)
Task Orienting (Chap. 7)
Demand Control (Chap. 8)
Limit Maintenance (Chap. 9)

3
Establishing Direction
a. Setting goals, priorities, and limits
b. Detail management

4
Maintaining Control
a. **Active concentration**
b. **Stress—and distress management**

FOCUSING ON GOALS

Once you establish clear direction in your program, you are on the path to becoming a successful time manager. But as you strive to reach your goals, interruptions, or pressures, can prevent carefully organized plans from being fulfilled. To successfully manage time, you must prepare yourself to overcome these deterrents and to continue focusing clearly on your goals. You need to retain control over your coaching environment. In this chapter, you will learn about two techniques which can add control to your day: active concentration and conscious distress management.

Concentration

Sarah and Frank do not have time or make the time to plan. They are unable to step back and evaluate their programs because they are so frequently interrupted. Concentration is impossible under these conditions. Sarah creates this environment for herself, and Frank creates it for others; thus, both have eliminated concentration as a useful time management tool.

Without the habit of self-induced concentration, Sarah and Frank give away their real time and rely instead on mythical time. When they do get down to finishing a project, they are under such external pressure that clear, careful thought becomes impossible. The results of this pressure are carelessly completed assignments and an ACORN environment. Pressured coaches, instead of concentrating on what really needs to be done, pressure those around them.

The experience of others who regularly give their work full commitment and intensity well before deadlines contradicts what Sarah, Frank, and the people around them have to endure. They have discovered that minutes can be used intelligently and on high-priority work, that colleagues can be asked to wait or come back later, and that doors can be closed. From these actions emerges a sense of purpose that translates into a determination to finish work quickly.

Like detail management, concentration becomes a useful time management tool when three changes take place:

1. Individuals such as Sarah develop a personal concentration routine and find ways to use it selectively each day.

2. Disruptors such as Frank become more sensitive to others' need for privacy.

3. People who work together establish traditions that allow for concentration through increased respect for the privacy of others.

Let us discuss the first change in behavior—developing a concentration routine.

Developing a Concentration Routine

Sarah is always telling her athletes to concentrate. "Watch the ball," she shouts on the practice field. "See the play in your head before you start," she advises during scrimmages and game huddles. "Focus on your goal" is another of her suggestions, for she is convinced that concentration is critical in mentally preparing for a successful performance. She knows from personal experience how effective this form of intensity can be. When she has time, Sarah often works with individual athletes who have difficulty concentrating. She will point out how by increasing their attention, they will improve their performance.

The value of applying these same methods of concentration to her own tasks off the field has not occurred to Sarah. While she can motivate herself for competition or some other enjoyable activity, she finds it hard to get excited about paperwork. But completing these assignments is critical to the success of her athletic program. Sarah and others battered by external and self-imposed interruptions need to blow a mental whistle and give concentration a chance. Coaches who try the following exercise often find that active and purposeful concentration contributes significantly to personal productivity.

A Concentration Exercise

Little time or effort is involved in making a concentration routine part of your day. It is easy to transfer the same attention you regularly devote to practice and competition to your program administration if you follow these three sequential steps:

1. Recall
2. Experimentation
3. Regular application

Recall

Recall requires thinking about what actually happens to you when concentrating. Consider activities other than athletics; for example, reading a good book, painting, sewing, cooking, playing a musical instrument, or singing can all stimulate heightened levels of attention. What activity absorbs your total concentration? Note the activity and how it makes you feel. Take a moment to consider when you concentrate most easily and most often. Here are some examples of activities and possible feelings:

Activity	Outcome (How you felt)
Reading	Totally involved
Painting	Relaxed
Playing an instrument	Able to hear the note in my mind before playing it

When an individual is focused on a single activity, researchers note the following:

- Activity receives full and complete attention; what was done before or might be coming next loses its importance.
- The environment is blocked out, eliminating any perceptions of noise or other distractions.
- The individual is self-confident and positive about doing well and tells him or herself so.
- A mental picture of success appears, heightening determination and self-confidence.
- Separation from the environment occurs; the individual blends into the task, increasing the intensity and euphoria associated with its accomplishment.
- A "flow," or attachment, develops between the individual and the activity; stopping becomes difficult.

Recalling the effects of concentration counters the battered mind. Using recall, Sarah, for example, could focus her attention on seeing one task to completion and be less controlled by what remains to be done.

Experimentation

Experimentation occurs when recall stimulates enthusiasm about the usefulness of concentration for boosting individual productivity. Everyone is a little unique. People concentrate better on different tasks at certain times and in special places. To determine what combination of these three factors works best for you, do the following:

1. *Identify* two or three relatively short tasks you now do well. Routine but not boring activities are best. Sarah, for example, might fill out registration forms or compose recruiting letters. She does these well when she has time.

2. *Pick* one or two periods during the day when your energy is high and interruptions are less likely; for example, early in the day either at home or the office, or just as most people leave for lunch.

3. *Determine* at least two locations, one at work and another at home, where you may be able to complete tasks with fewer disturbances.

"Locking in" on an Activity

Try the following five-step process. It will help you to "lock in" on completing one activity at a time. With practice, your concentration skills will improve greatly regardless of the attractiveness of the activity. Before you begin, first identify a specific time, place, and task. These elements will enhance concentration. You may find that you do not need all the five steps to concentrate.

The Five-Step Process for "Locking In"

Selection of task, time, and place enhances concentration. Once this is done, you are ready for the five-step process that leads to "locking in" on one task irrespective of its appeal.

1. *Develop a frame of mind.* The frame is a message to yourself that clarifies the importance of concentrating on one task. It increases your motivation because it clarifies your purpose, reducing any tendency to procrastinate. Motivation increases as a purpose becomes clear. For example, imagine the pleasure of having unpleasant work completed and being able to relax afterward.

2. *Relax for a moment.* A moment of relaxation helps to shut out the environment and to focus your mind on the one task to be completed.

3. *Develop a mental picture.* Imagine yourself actually doing the task. This enables you to see possible problems and helps you to "visualize" the final product. It also helps focus your concentration on the single task.

4. *Take a few deep breaths.* Athletes do this before a competitive event. It helps them to focus completely on their immediate goal. It can also help you to realize your goals.

5. *Establish "flow" with a directing message.* "Flow" describes what happens when task and person blend together when a momentum is established. Talking to oneself helps create flow by heightening self-motivation and directing it to a specific task. For example, you could say, "I'm going to finish this practice plan this morning," or "Before noon, I'll write all recruiting letters."

Gradually, you will find yourself able to expand the number and difficulty of tasks you are able to address. You may also discover that the results of improved concentration motivate you to find even more uninterrupted time each day.

Regular Application

Dedicated concentrators report five daily benefits from developing a routine.

1. *High-priority assignments are given single-minded attention.* This requires closing doors, asking some visitors to come back later, and even finding hiding places away from the flow of traffic. Concentrators let potential interrupters know they need some momentary privacy.

2. *Improved concentration results in less task hopping.* "If interrupted in the middle of a letter, I ask a visitor to wait for a moment," a school administrator observed. "Finishing just one sentence helps me return to the unfinished letter once the visit is over." Other managers learn to put phone calls temporarily on hold. The request for "just one minute until I finish" increases productive use of minutes and makes interruptions seem less jarring as a result.

3. *Less reliance on mythical time* is the third benefit of concentration. "Concentrators" see minutes as gifts of time that can be used to write a letter, to read an important notice, *or* to review plans. With these minutes, concentrators accomplish a great deal. They are organized to take advantage of unexpected periods which become available. If a meeting begins late or an appointment ends early, the minutes can be used to good advantage.

4. *Reduced concern over what remains to be done* is the fourth benefit of the ability to concentrate. With the single-minded focus that concentration produces, concentrators are mentally doing one task at a time. Digressive thinking becomes less common because one task has a tenacious hold over their attention. Consequently, little time is spent brooding or worrying about remaining tasks.

5. *Concentrators become better listeners.* Sarah heard only about one-third of the conversation with her troubled athlete. She was busy panicking over what she still had to do before practice. If her routine had included active concentration, she would have done more in the morning. Then in the afternoon, she would have been able to listen and perhaps offer good advice to her distressed athlete.

Coaches like Sarah need to recognize the value of improving their concentration skills and to try to incorporate these skills into their daily routine. Coaches who see how much this ability to concentrate contributes to athletic performance should recognize its value in an office setting. The same intensity and internal motivation critical to success in competition can be used to complete many tasks in the office.

Using concentration seems like a common sense solution to a productivity problem. Unfortunately, not everyone behaves as expected. For example, coaches like Frank are insensitive to the impact of their behavior on others, behavior that can only be changed with some honest prodding from others.

Learning to be Sensitive to Others' Needs for Privacy

"You, you're driving me crazy" is the opening line to an old romantic ballad. In it, a lovestruck suitor describes his mental distress and inability to function. Assistant coaches, athletes, secretaries, and a host of others would like to say the same thing to Frank. For various reasons, however, they do not and Frank goes on making concentration difficult if not impossible for others. His behavior suggests that privacy rights do not exist.

The best way to sensitize Frank to others' needs is to point out the impact of his behavior. Diplomacy rather than a general indictment of his behavior is the better approach. Below are some sample statements that can help to sensitize others to a need for privacy.

- "Can you come back later? I'm having a hard time concentrating on this report."

- "I'm sorry but I don't have time to discuss a new idea now—details have to come first!"

- "Excuse me, but I have to have this work done by 10:00, and I don't have anytime to talk now. Can I get back to you later on today?"

- "Sorry, I don't have time for a story now!"

When candor is possible, and it is in many public and private settings, "honesty is the best policy." Through its use, individuals like Frank Adams may begin to realize that privacy is necessary and should be respected.

Unfortunately, there is no guarantee that Frank or others in leadership positions will become more sensitive to the effect of their actions on others. Furthermore, your position in an organization can certainly interfere with honesty. You may not be able to successfully change such behavior, either because some individuals are unaware of how their behavior upsets other people, or because you are not in a position to be so open. Under these circumstances, you might suggest another concentration technique.

Establishing a Concentration Tradition

Employees at Marriott, Delta Airlines, and IBM have a "quiet hour" two to three times a week when relative silence and privacy are to be observed. Although this hour cannot be strictly enforced all the time, it has become a tradition in these and other organizations. Employees at all levels report getting far more done because of that hour and also discover they have increased respect for time as a valuable and shared resource.

Major corporations are not alone in their respect for time. Smaller public organizations are recognizing the need for concentration as a part of each day's routine. Local governments, social service agencies, school district offices, and other organizations have introduced some new concentration traditions. Nothing elaborate is needed to create such a tradition. In fact, single words or phrases such as the following can remind people who work together that concentration is necessary.

- *Whoa*—a moment of thought that should precede dropping in on another person: Is it appropriate now or can the visit be postponed or cancelled?

- *In writing*—a suggestion that a note may be better than a visit.
- *Set times*—for individuals who are in regular contact; they should stay in touch but at prearranged times each day except for emergencies.
- *Really necessary*—for meetings. Before a meeting is set, its purpose must be clear: no purpose, no meeting.

Respect for each other and the need for privacy are the reasons why these reminders are effective. People in the same environment who want to do a good job have agreed to establish a few simple traditions that ensure some privacy.

Consider what a tradition of concentration and privacy could contribute to your athletic program. In an environment where interruptions are the rule, capable people do not have time to think about and then effectively handle so-called "minor" details. Unless you ask others to understand and to support your need for concentration, you will probably have little success in doing it yourself. Sarah, for example, will not experience much progress until she decides to close her door and to ask visitors to come back later. Then she must get agreement from those in the program to respect the meaning of a closed door.

With a privacy tradition that allows individuals to concentrate, Sarah and others would be in control of their environment instead of constantly struggling. Changing attitudes and establishing a new tradition will not be easy. However, given the consequences of the ACORN environment and the battered mind, the effort is certainly worthwhile. Athletes who concentrate in practice and in competition tend to be more successful than those who do not. You can achieve that same success by improving your concentration off the field.

STRESS

For many coaches, the attraction of a book on time management is the hope of discovering ways of eliminating stress caused by poor time management. Harmful stress is a result of the ACORN environment and the battered mind. The chaos, the pressure, and the exhaustion stress produces can limit your ability to function. How stress can help as well as harm you will be discussed in this section. You will see how time pressures and work overload cause stress, and how you can learn to deal with stress on a lifelong basis.

What Is Stress?

Not all stress is harmful. How improved concentration contributes to daily accomplishment was explained in the previous section. According to University of Chicago psychologist Mihali Csikszentmihalyi, concentration is a form of self-induced and self-controlled stress called *eustress*. Eustress is a positive form of stress, whereas other forms are not; psychologists call these other forms *distress*. You can think of stress on a continuum made up of six stages that produce increasingly harmful consequences:

Stage 1

At Stage 1 is eustress, which involves a mild stress usually accompanied by feelings of great zest, acute perception, and excessive nervous energy. Individuals at this stage find they have an ability to accomplish more work than usual. The pleasant feelings associated with eustress can make it addicting. But human energy is finite, and too much of this concentration can exhaust energy reserves, leaving an individual vulnerable to the next stage where distress begins.

Stage 2

This is where the unpleasant effects of stress begin. Energy reserves no longer last through the day, but diminish after lunch or early in the afternoon. Occasional disturbances of the bowel and stomach functions, along with heart flutters, can appear. Typical reactions also include tightness of muscles in the back and around the skull together with a feeling of being unable to relax.

Stage 3

Individuals at this stage have more pronounced fatigue, as well as greater disturbances of bowel functions, stomach troubles, and muscle tightening. Increased feelings of tenseness, sleep disturbances, and feelings of faintness without fainting are present.

Stage 4

For individuals at Stage 4, each day seems difficult. Activities that formerly were pleasant, including conversations with friends, become trying. Sleep is disturbed, a fear that cannot be pinpointed is present, and concentration is all but impossible.

Stage 5

This stage begins a profound deepening of the previous symptoms. Extreme fatigue, difficulty in managing all but fairly simple tasks, great disturbances of bowel and stomach functions, and pervasive feelings of fear are common.

Stage 6

This stage lies at the extreme end of the stress continuum and can produce terrifying symptoms. Common ones include a pounding heart and panic caused by adrenalin reactions, gasping for breath, or uncontrolled trembling, shivering, and sweating. Numbness or tingling sensations in the hands and feet often occur. Exhaustion sets in, and even the simplest tasks seem to require too much energy.

Where each stage lies on the stress continuum is shown below. How fast and how far you move up the continuum depends upon your environment and upon your tolerance for stress. You have already seen how you can change your environment. The latter part of this chapter will discuss how you can increase your tolerance for stress. But first, how can you get stress to work for you?

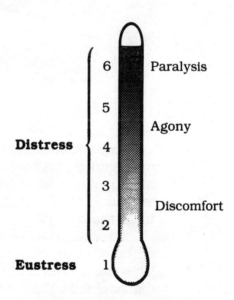

The Stages of Stress

Eustress

All of us have experienced eustress at some time, generally when we needed to accomplish a great deal in a specific period of time. In these instances, we have mentally prepared ourselves to do our best. Athletes are able to improve their performances by concentrating on single events for a short period of time. As good examples of eustress, the following athletes have noted in television interviews how concentration helps them to improve competitive performance:

• Greg Louganis, the diving champion, talks to himself about the importance of each dive to build a necessary level of intensity before he climbs onto the diving board.

• Billie Jean King focuses on each point in a tennis game to block out what happened previously in her match and to give all her attention to one serve or return shot.

• Kareem Abdul Jabar concentrates on relaxing before a game so he can plan how to deal with the opposing team's center.

• Pete Rose relaxes before his turn at bat, thinks about the pitches he would like, and then focuses his attention on getting a hit.

Of course, eustress is not restricted to athletes. Successful managers report how they focus their attention on an upcoming appointment or meeting. In addition to preparing written plans, they mentally review what will happen and how to do the best job possible on each occasion.

Executive secretaries, administrative assistants, and others who coordinate major conferences, reports, and projects use a similar kind of concentration, focusing on detail management. They think intensely about what must be done to handle each responsibility and write out important items they might forget.

Slowing down enough to think through each project, competition, or practice produces a self-confidence that comes from knowing exactly where you are going and how you will get there. Self-confidence, together with the eustress that initiated it, can motivate you to continue to work efficiently, without distress. Unfortunately, too many individuals do not know how to make stress work for them. They cannot or will not control the pressure on them, they do not slow down, and they do not take the time to relax. As a result, these individuals are less able to function effectively.

Distress

Do you remember how fast Sarah moved from Stage 2 to Stage 4 on the stress continuum? On Monday, she was already near panic even before the afternoon practice began. As the week progressed, stress continued to increase. Although Frank handled stress a little differently, his approach was just as ineffective. Frank's procrastination, last-minute pressure, and unjustified blaming caused his assistants to move rapidly up the stress continuum.

Stress is a common phenomenon in sports. Coaches and athletes are often under so much pressure to win: The pressure from parents, sponsoring agencies, and fans can all serve to make sports exceedingly stressful. The inherent uncertainty of the outcome in sports, sometimes regardless of effort, only increases the pressure. Because sports are so naturally stressful, it is up to coaches to manage and to eliminate stress in those areas they can control. Research on stress emphasizes the crucial role coaches play in keeping distress levels as low as possible. If coaches feel overly stressed, their exhaustion, negativism, tension, and reduced self-confidence can influence the entire team.

Coaches and players inevitably experience some nervousness as they prepare for competition. While coaches, like players, use eustress to increase their self-confidence and emphasize excellent performance, coaches who assume unrealistic workloads are almost certain to experience distress.

For example, Dick Vermeil, recently retired coach of the Philadelphia Eagles, is an individual who apparently took on too much in pursuit of success. During the season, he devoted himself completely to the team, engaging in dozens of activities without respite: He organized practices and prepared game plans, he constantly studied films of his and other teams, and he had the coaching staff meet with him for long hours. Although the Eagles were successful, Vermeil suffered increasing exhaustion. He resigned because of too much pressure caused by his unceasing drive for success. With great candor on national TV, Vermeil explained his surprising decision to resign.

Vermeil's colleague on CBS, John Madden, also left coaching for the same reason. Unable to control the pressures on them, these two capable individuals were forced to make decisions which shortened their coaching careers but which probably lengthened their lives. You may have read about other successful coaches, men and women alike, in college and high school sports, who also stopped coaching because of constant external and internal pressure to improve. For example:

- The women's field hockey coach at a Big Ten university who felt she couldn't say no to requests for assistance from colleagues because she was the last person hired. Her workload grew until she left for a less demanding position.

- The swimming coach at a major club in California, who could not get necessary assistance from parents, decided all the pressure had been placed on him, tired of it, and resigned his position.

- The Illinois high school basketball coach with a 10-year plus winning record who tired of fans expecting miracles each season and so asked to be relieved.

Because of pressure from a too heavy load or a win-at-all costs attitude, these coaches pushed themselves to the point of physical and mental exhaustion. What these and other coaches like them did not realize is that their goals were unrealistic. Lacking realistic goals, they worked feverishly to achieve impossible ones. Instead of being pleased with reasonable individual and team progress, they were frustrated by their failures. In their rush to achieve, they forgot about organization and time management. They forgot to plan, to prioritize, to concentrate, to give themselves a rest. Like Sarah, they spent all their time running, reacting, and agreeing to do more. Their rush to achieve too much, in effect, ensured that they would achieve too little: They simply became too tired and too stressed to continue.

Managing Distress

If you recognize yourself in these stories, then you need to learn how to handle and perhaps how to reduce stress either in yourself or in those with whom you work. Distress control is possible, just as eliminating the ACORN environment is possible. Whenever you feel under pressure, apply the following four-step process. It will help you reduce the negative consequences of stress.

1. Identify the causes of distress.
2. Identify possible solutions.
3. Emphasize the positive.
4. Respond rationally.

Identify the Causes of Distress

Identifying the causes of distress is an essential first step to managing it. Too often we experience tension that if left to fester can begin to control us. Often several things working together can produce unhealthy stress levels and make identification of a single source difficult. Listed below are eight common causes of distress to help with this identification process. Examples of typical coaching situations which can cause distress are also included.

Constant and Unexpected Changes

- "This revised meet registration procedure is effective immediately."
- "Beginning at noon you will be on temporary reassignment."
- "The starting time has been changed; the team will have to leave three hours earlier."

Increasing Demands on Time

- "Please take on these three additional duties as part of your regular work load."

- "From now on cross-country is your responsibility, as well as track."
- "Please plan to attend all daily staff meetings."
- "Could you help explain to these two new employees their in-school assignments!"

Lack of Guidance in Making Decisions or Dealing With New Assignments

- "Here is the problem, now go to it."
- "I'll be out of town for the next week and expect a recruiting report to be finished when I return."
- "There isn't time for explanation."
- "Everybody understand? Fine, can I expect the answers by noon?"

Relationships With Others

- "All I ever hear about are her problems."
- "The principal doesn't listen even when he claims to."
- "Can't those two ever be quiet?"
- "I guess we have to work with Mr. 'No' now."

Repressed Feelings and Emotions

- "Nobody really listens to my ideas."
- "He shouldn't have gotten the athletic director's position."
- "Nobody understands the pressure I'm under."

Family-Oriented Difficulties

- "Our money runs out before the month does."
- "We don't communicate as much as we should."
- "The children just won't listen."

My Work Environment
- Too cramped.
- Too noisy.
- No privacy.
- Constant interruptions.

Time Management Problems
- Allowing priorities to remain unclear.
- Poor planning.
- Taking on too much.
- Procrastinating and creating pressure on self and others.
- Doing work others should.

You can make up your own lists and use them as a guide, or you may want to involve your co-workers in identifying causes of distress. Often, by openly discussing the causes of pressure in your program, you, as a group can begin to identify specific ways to deal with these pressures.

Identify Possible Solutions

Many times, difficulties can be minimized or eliminated through discussion. For example, if Sarah had discussed the pressure she felt by being constantly accessible, the others might have agreed to leave her alone at certain times. Instead, Sarah suffered in silence.

Unfortunately, some pressure-causing problems will not go away because changes or additional responsibilities may be a part of your job. One way to lessen the pressure of a change is to view it as a challenge. Although this does not eliminate the pressure, it may help reduce it as you prove to yourself each day that the challenge can be met.

Suppose a valued assistant becomes ill and cannot work for a week or more. You and others fill in, taking on some of the assistant's priority assignments. Some activities are put aside. This is a common challenge all of us face and usually handle quite well. We also deal with arrangements that break down, equipment which does not arrive on time, and weather that forces games or meets to be cancelled. Instead of collapsing, we figure out rational ways to handle each situation.

You must use this same approach with other causes of distress. Instead of believing events run your life, assess what you can do to lessen their impact. With a colleague, develop realistic solutions to changes. If you had to leave 3 hours earlier for a competition, you would have to evaluate the situation and adapt your plans accordingly. Handling new tasks or reorganizing old ones is no different. Every day we all cope with change, demands on our time, and many other possible causes of distress. Recognizing that we have the ability to cope, we are more likely to use this ability regularly and confidently.

By identifying causes and solutions, you are taking an important first step in managing the distress in your life. Just as setting goals can become a habit, so can dealing with the various pressures in your life. Even handling some temporary pressure is an important way of learning how to cope.

Keep in mind that sources of distress do not remain static, for the causes you identify this week or this month may be entirely different from those you experience in the future. In healthy organizations, managers take the lead in looking at causes of distress and undue pressure. They hold regular discussions in which the entire group can try to make the environment better for everyone. Logical ways to minimize pressure emerge from collective action. Once you have begun to identify the causes of stress and search for possible solutions, the next step is to emphasize your achievements.

Emphasize the Positive

Self-respect is an essential element in distress control. Your confidence erodes as you lose control, and tasks not finished or errors made only seem to emphasize personal failure. You can avoid feelings of inadequacy by taking one or more of the following steps.

Be Proud of Yourself

At the end of each day, mentally list what you have accomplished (and make a written list for regular review). A "to do" list can be checked and work done erased. One high school coach told me that throwing away his completed list at the end of each day makes him feel successful.

Recognize Your Physical and Mental Limits

Learn to stop when you need rest. Find time to slow down and do not push yourself to exhaustion level.

Select a Hobby or Pastime Other Than Coaching

You can experience a sense of relief by woodworking, painting, or cooking. Hobbies or recreational activities provide a mental haven during busy times.

Make Time Each Day to Relax

Relaxation, not collapse, allows you to rebuild energy by slowing down. Unless relaxation becomes a part of your daily routine, it most likely will not take place.

Incorporate Some Form of Exercise Into Your Daily Routine

Studies have shown that self-concept improves as physical fitness increases.

Do Not Become Pressured by People and Events

The questionnaire on page 72 can help you evaluate the level of pressure you feel. Circle the number which most accurately represents your response to the statement.

HOW PRESSURED ARE YOU?

1. Do minor problems and disappointments get under your skin and rile you more than they should?

1	2	3	4	5
Rarely		Sometimes		Often

2. Are you finding it hard to get along with people? Are people having trouble getting along with you?

1	2	3	4	5
Rarely		Sometimes		Often

3. Have you found that you are not getting much of a kick anymore from the things you used to enjoy: for example, watching a basketball game, fishing or camping, seeing a movie?

1	2	3	4	5
Rarely		Sometimes		Often

4. Do your anxieties haunt you? Are you unable to shut them out of your mind?

1	2	3	4	5
Rarely		Sometimes		Often

5. Are you now scared of people and situations that never used to bother you?

1	2	3	4	5
Rarely		Sometimes		Often

6. Have you noticed that you are becoming suspicious of people around you, even your friends?

1	2	3	4	5
Rarely		Sometimes		Often

7. Is there the feeling that you are being trapped?

1	2	3	4	5
Rarely		Sometimes		Often

8. Do you feel inadequate, just not good enough to hack it?

1	2	3	4	5
Rarely		Sometimes		Often

The higher your total score, the more susceptible you are to harmful pressure. A dangerous total would be beyond 30. Admitting you sometimes feel some level of tension is normal as long as you have methods to reduce the level.

Keeping up your confidence and fitness belong in your inner ring of highest priority activities. Remember, your attitude affects your entire program; if you sink under pressure, it will too. The fourth step for reducing stress is to remain calm and attempt to think rationally.

Respond
Rationally

You are given less than an hour to prepare an important statement. Three people with problems come in within minutes to see you, all wanting answers immediately. An assistant coach cannot make it to practice. In situations like these, tension mounts quickly, and the pressure you feel can create some irrational feelings of inadequacy.

As coach, you are expected to act calmly and effectively, not with anger, panic, or paralysis. Your first reaction to any sudden demand should be to take a few moments to think about the situation and how you will handle it. To accomplish this, do the following:

1. Temporarily reorder your priorities and put aside other work.

2. Clear an area so you can concentrate on just one task.

3. Develop a plan for preparing the statement or handling the work of the assistant coach.

4. Push yourself to complete the work using the concentration routine suggested earlier in this chapter.

These actions demonstrate you are in control of a potentially disruptive situation. When the work is done, you can look back with pride on what your rational response produced.

I'm often asked about situations when three people want answers immediately. As several coaches have pointed out, each of us has but one mouth and one mind. Therefore, only one person can get an answer at a time; the other two will have to wait. You must determine which person takes precedence on the basis of the problem each presents. Once you have made this decision, you have established a plan of action and should give your total attention to the first question. Initially, you may not find this commitment easy; it will certainly test your concentration skills. However, you should recognize that it is the only realistic response and act with this conviction.

As you handle these and other situations, you will develop the skills of *crisis sensitivity* and *crisis memory*. These will help you to manage time and potential distress. Crisis sensitivity is simply a recognition that the unexpected is really an everyday occurrence. In our complex world, problems occur no matter how well-managed the person or organization. If you are alert to the problems associated with planning a major competition, registering athletes, or arranging a trip, you will be less surprised by unexpected events. You will also have time left to deal with problems because you will realize the need to set limits on your workload.

Coaches who use these techniques remember how similar problems were handled in the past. They may have prepared a list of details, phone numbers of people to call, or logical alternatives. By relying on written records, these coaches are not handicapped by poor memories. Their written record is their crisis memory, allowing them to be more relaxed because they know that valuable information is readily available.

Distress Management as a Lifelong Activity

Distress management is not something you do only when things get out of control. The ability to plan, to discuss, and to react rationally comes from an inner calm and clarity. There are many ways to control distress on a regular basis; the following six have been suggested by the National Association for Mental Health (NAMH) as a starting point:

Ventilate

Let out some of the steam by talking through problems with trusted individuals. They could be members of your immediate family, a longtime friend, or a clergyman. To whom you talk is not important; what *is* important is that he or she has your trust and a willing ear. Acording to the NAMH, ventilating relieves the strain, puts worries in clearer light, and can lead to rational and realistic solutions.

Move Away

Take yourself physically away from the source of the pressure. Pressure builds in the most well-run organizations, causing you to tighten up. Even a momentary departure from the scene of action for a cup of coffee, a brisk walk, or a chat, can change your perspective. Time away gives you a chance to catch your breath and to regain the balance that pressure has a way of shaking.

Sweat Away the Anger

Pressure usually starts working internally, causing headaches, heartburn, or other mental and physical symptoms. Physical activity can help to release tension. To some extent, anger and frustration can be sweated out of the system. To his credit, Frank found time for a workout at midday. Given the intensity of her morning, Sarah should have considered a similar break.

Move On

If you run into a block, do not let it become more significant by fussing or fretting over your inability to get past it. Put the project aside for awhile and return later. NAMH research has shown, you will generally find renewed strength, and a solution may emerge during the break. If you have had difficulty with an assignment in the morning, consider returning to it in the afternoon, or try tackling only a very small piece of a problem.

Avoid Perfection

Too many capable individuals are less effective because they constantly seek perfection. They expect a great deal of themselves and feel they have failed if they cannot immediately produce a perfect solution. Distress can be reduced if you orient yourself toward what you *did* accomplish rather than what you did not.

Give In

Do not stand your ground all of the time, even in those situations where you are completely certain of your position's merit. Yielding occasionally, according to the NAMH, reduces much strain on the nervous system and pays off in better all-round relations. Always fighting to win increases tension and makes opponents of colleagues.

In considering these six suggestions identify what works for you and mentally record these solutions for later use. By your example, you may encourage others to do the same.

SUMMARY AND RECOM-MENDATIONS

Excessive pressure can batter minds and lead to mental and physical exhaustion. Pressures can easily distract you from focusing on the direction you have established for your program. Improving your skills of concentration will help you control the pressures in your coaching environment. Coaches are naturally susceptible to the harmful effects of stress because of desires to win at all costs, of setting unrealistic goals, and of failing to organize for consistent accomplishment. By building a healthy working environment, you and others in your program will be able to accomplish the following:

1. Evaluate the total program to assess progress, spot problems, and make necessary changes.

2. Find time to concentrate so that "real," not "mythical" time is used to finish work well before deadlines approach.

3. Sensitize those who interrupt to the impact of their behavior on others.

4. Develop a concentration/privacy tradition that enables individuals to work alone as much as possible.

5. Remember that not all stress is harmful. *Eustress* can improve your performance and increase your concentration.

6. Avoid *distress*. As stress levels are permitted to intensify, the effect becomes increasingly unpleasant until individuals are unable to function.

7. Control distress by following the four-step process of (a) identifying the causes, (b) identifying possible solutions, (c) emphasizing the positive, and (d) responding rationally to potentially difficult situations.

8. Manage distress by using those techniques already described as well as ventilating, moving away from the source of pressure, exercising, moving on, avoiding perfection, and giving in on occasions.

9. Recognize that distress management is a lifelong activity.

By establishing direction and maintaining control over your environment, all coaches can improve their time management. But to become totally effective, some "individualization" must take place. The need to relate time management techniques to your own unique personality will be examined in Part 2.

PART 2
Time Management Techniques in Practice

CREATING A PERSONAL RECIPE FOR EFFECTIVE TIME MANAGEMENT

A few years ago, a manager in a large public agency showed what often happens when time management skills are pitted against personal habits. Six weeks after presenting a time management seminar at that agency, I returned for a follow-up session. As various approaches were being reviewed, this manager related that none were working for her.

"None?" I asked with obvious embarrassment.

"Not the way you described," she responded. "They wouldn't work in my position so I made some changes. Now I have my own recipe!"

Her comments started a spirited discussion about personal time management recipes. One person in the group compared time management to the preparation of homemade chili: Fine touches make each person's version a little different.

There is no single "right" way to manage time. A high degree of personalization takes place in the use of specific time management techniques. Some individuals lean toward complex procedures like detailed schedules and extensive self and staff reminders, while others work best with only a quickly scrawled series of notes. Through a process of trial and error, each of us becomes committed to a few approaches that work best for us. We, in essence, create our own recipes for time management.

Everyone has a personal style of management. Even disorganization represents a style. So, too, does waiting until the last minute to work feverishly under pressure. When individuals make improvements in time management, they complement and add to techniques already established. Consider these improvements similar to the bark around a tree. The bark surrounds and reinforces an already established core. Whatever new approaches you choose must fit around an organizing core already in place; in other words, you must use time management techniques that fit your personality, or you most likely will not use them at all.

LOGICALLY ADDING TO WHAT WORKS

Bob, a local businessman and part-time tennis coach, asked me to help him improve his time management. He felt his lack of organization was affecting his success in both business and coaching. Bob was extremely energetic and had many good ideas, but he tended to overload himself, hop from task to task, and spend more time on details than priorities.

We found a few minutes to talk after he had a lesson with a young player named Richard. Bob explained how he was building on Richard's natural athletic and tennis ability. "His forehand is his best stroke, so I'm working on that first." Bob planned to work on Richard's serve next because this was another skill Richard had picked up quickly. Backhand, lobs, and net play would follow later to expand Richard's overall game. At every lesson, Bob reinforced what worked. Richard finished each lesson feeling he was a little stronger in one or two aspects of tennis play.

Bob understood the similarity between his approach to tennis instruction and mine to improving his time management. "But I can't see the same kind of results Richard does when he hits a winning shot," he admitted. "Those successes encourage him to go on, learn more, and practice and remain excited about the game!"

Improving time management did not appear to have the same "emotional" appeal to Bob. To capture Bob's motivation, I suggested a building-block approach based on three techniques he periodically used:

- A weekly plan which emphasized business goals, ordering supplies, scheduling part-time help at the tennis club, paying certain bills, *and* analyzing where the business could grow.
- Prelesson planning for every individual and group lesson.
- Occasional short periods alone in his office to do the work he had identified on his weekly plan—Bob rarely used this technique preferring to leave his door open and suffered constant interruptions.

I suggested he use these three techniques *habitually* rather than periodically for at least one month. To increase that likelihood, I encouraged Bob to write these three techniques on two 3" × 5" cards, placing them in prominent locations in his office and home.

Then we discussed building on the basis of these three strengths similar to the way he was teaching Richard to play tennis. His weekly plan could help him clarify goals by simply adding a couple of lines under the heading "Goals For This Week." This simple addition encouraged Bob to think about what he could become—a successful tennis coach-businessman.

Another modification built on his prelesson planning. An experienced tennis coach had once told Bob how he obtained all of his students by referral from satisfied players or parents. "With a busy teaching schedule, you can easily forget about individual student needs and lose the personal touch," the coach told Bob, "and that personal touch plus your teaching ability is the motivation which keeps students coming and staying."

Improved planning was the solution for other problems Bob was experiencing; these included training new part-time help, planning club tournaments, organizing special activities for junior members, and publicizing weekend tennis parties to attract potential new members. In an earlier conversation, Bob had mentioned that when he organized a lesson, he visualized both the student and what he wanted that person to learn. "I concentrate on both, then identify what should be done," he said. The same approach was relevant to training a new employee or planning a club event. "Concentrate on what that person should know and how you can make it clear," I suggested. "In your mind's eye, visualize what the employee should be able to do."

It is important to remember that these suggestions were made gradually, similar to Bob's work with Richard. Both had a chance to absorb and to try out a limited amount of new information and experience the pleasure of accomplishment.

Recently, Bob and I began to discuss his irregular use of time alone. The daily calendar on his desk is blank except for lessons and other planned club events. I suggested he pencil in "time alone" on his calendar, making it a daily event. Bob is now in the process of doing this.

The key to Bob's success is the logical addition of modifications or expansions to what already works. He remains motivated because he can see the relationship between these alterations and the improvements in his program which include:

- More time to plan major club events because he has trained his staff to handle work he used to do.
- A slight but evident increase in new members.
- Fewer times when popular items are out-of-stock.
- A "feeling" he is more in control of what happens each day.

Bob feels that the steps he has taken to improve his time management have produced significant results. He continues to refine his organizational methods by trying out new techniques and by evaluating their effectiveness. You must do the same to develop your own personalized system of time management.

TIME MANAGEMENT TECHNIQUES

Through research, five clusters of time management techniques have been identified: goal setting, routine planning, task orienting, demand control, and limit maintenance. In practice, these techniques tend to be interrelated. No one uses skills from only one of these categories. Yet it is clear that successful time managers do have specific strengths concentrated in one or other of the technique areas. For personal reasons, you may find one of these clusters especially attractive and relevant for supplementing your existing organizational techniques.

Goal setting gives a clear sense of direction. It also provides well-defined criteria for measuring progress. The commitment to a clear direction and the existence of clear progress measures, produce a desire for excellence. Goal-oriented individuals plan for the long term and are regularly thinking ahead. A sense of where one wants to be is their trigger for activity. However, these individuals do not lose sight of the present, and are constantly searching for new challenges.

Routine planning provides a structure or framework for getting work done. Before action begins, a plan must be made. Time is assigned to certain regular responsibilities. Special projects are analyzed and time is allotted to them. In order for the routine to be effective, those with a planning orientation attempt to manage interruptions and control paperwork. Low-priority tasks are handled as quickly as possible. A person with these skills often finds that a routine is the motivator to begin work and to stay on track.

Task orienting helps develop ways to concentrate on one task at a time. Immediate job responsibilities take precedence over more interesting, but less significant activities. The details of each task are not forgotten, and nothing is too small for attention. Individuals who are task oriented rarely make assumptions about details. With this emphasis comes a willingness to remove distractions from an office or to find a distraction-free environment. Pacing oneself to complete work on time and an ability to follow up with others are task-oriented skills. Rather than being motivated by a long-term goal, task-oriented individuals get their motivation from the task at hand.

Demand control means that high priorities get immediate attention. That attitude is part of a calm and deliberate reaction to events. Crisis control is very important to these individuals; some develop a memory of past difficulties so similar ones can be addressed more easily in the future. They separate legitimate demands on their time from those which are inappropriate. Individuals who must handle many demands will often make themselves less available because withdrawing regularly is important to them. Meetings, a form of demand, are reduced in length. Responding to the highest priorities first is the force behind this orientation.

Limit maintenance is guided by a desire to maintain a

steady and manageable work output. Individuals in this group are careful not to push themselves beyond endurance levels. They establish a pace and try to keep to it. Delegation is important to them as is time for thought and self-renewal. Constant self-monitoring helps them to maintain an even pace. Effective and controlled communication plays a part in their style; staying in touch with others is part of this paced routine. The motivator and governor to people with this orientation is a pace that can be maintained.

The coaches you will meet in the next five chapters have developed their own time management recipes based principally on one of the five clusters of time management techniques. These coaches are described to show you how they selected specific techniques to supplement their existing skills and to help them control and direct their busy daily schedules. Try to notice how each coach has a *reason* for wanting to improve his or her use of time. Without motivation, it is difficult to make any substantial changes in our daily behavior. Identifying goals and planning how to achieve them gives us the motivation to persevere when it might be easier to give up.

As you read, decide whether any of techniques used by the five coaches could help you. In chapter 2 you were encouraged to develop reminder cards to focus your attention on the time management techniques you currently use. Since then, some new ideas may have inspired you to modify your original selection of techniques. Shown below is a revised version of the advice you were given earlier for constructing a personal recipe for successful time management. This list emphasizes the ongoing nature of the organizational processes which will bring direction and control to your athletic program.

- Write down techniques which already work on reminder index cards.
- Post them in visible locations and review them periodically.
- Select new techniques which you feel may improve your time use.
- Integrate only one or two new modifications at a time.
- Develop the habit of relating your successes to your reminder list.
- Review periodically and determine what really works.
- Add modifications to the reminder cards.

Remember, because you already have time management habits based on your personality, you will be able to make only minor modifications to your personal style, not substantial changes. You may add two, three, possibly even four variations or expansions to what you currently do. These additions can give you an important productivity boost and can bring more control to each day.

Chapter 5
Goals Above All

1
Time Management and Sports
a. Ineffective time management
b. The ACORN environment

2
Analyzing Time Use
a. Self-evaluation and self-monitoring
b. Personal time management recipes

3
Establishing Direction
a. Setting goals, priorities, and limits
b. Detail management

4
Maintaining Control
a. Active concentration
b. Stress—and distress management

5-9
Time Management Techniques in Practice
Goal Setting (Chap. 5)
Routine Planning (Chap. 6)
Task Orienting (Chap. 7)
Demand Control (Chap. 8)
Limit Maintenance (Chap. 9)

10
Starting and Maintaining Effective Time Management
a. Selecting and using techniques
b. Reaching out to others

IDENTIFYING GOALS: JOHN GIBBS

John Gibbs knew he wanted to coach even when he was in high school. "Sure I loved to play, but my talent was just average," John admits. "I was sixth, seventh, even eighth person, an important substitute. What was really exciting to me were the opportunities to help others develop. Teaching younger kids just seemed natural, as well as being rewarding and enjoyable."

With that attitude, John found time to become a volunteer basketball and track coach in high school and later in college. Besides assisting the basketball and track coaches, he worked with elementary school boys and girls. The more John coached, the more his enthusiasm for the profession grew.

After graduating from college, he obtained a combined teaching and coaching position at a small high school. In addition to his science classes, John was in charge of cross-country, basketball, and track. Other teachers coached, too, but none had quite his enthusiasm. John readily admitted he was a coach first and science teacher second.

In addition to being called "coach" at the high school, John was named athletic director by the other coaches. "It meant some additional work, mainly administration, but I actually enjoyed filling out forms and making the details come together," he said.

The more John coached, the more he knew this was his life's work. After 5 years at the high school, he obtained a coaching position at a small college in his local community. It was the next step in a carefully considered career plan.

"Obtained" is an important word in John's vocabulary. He is a very determined and purpose-driven young man. All his life, John has made events happen rather than hope they will magically occur. In one sense, John is fortunate because he has always known that coaching was the profession for him. Because of this, John was able to plan the steps in his coaching career. His next goal is achieving the athletic director's position at a nearby medium-sized university.

"I enjoy making things work. The athletic director's job at that university is something to shoot for. The institution is large, but not overpowering. And I'd still be able to coach track," John reasons.

John is so aware of his goal, he can easily identify milestones along the way. He uses these progress measures regularly and finds they enhance his motivation to organize and to produce a successful program.

GOAL SETTING

Everyday John sets his sights on reaching some milestone on the way to that sought-after head coaching and administrative position. It was this determination which led him to inquire about possible openings at the small college that eventually hired him. Persistence paid off for John in a very real way: He identified an important objective and kept after it.

John thinks about the steps he must take to reach his goals. "There are many distractions, and I want to stay away from most of them," he says. "Planning my life helps a great deal." John's sensitivity to distractions make him purposeful, and he also knows when to stop and enjoy life. One of his goals is to have a balanced life that includes time for his family and for himself.

Planning his life through clearly defined goals is the foundation for John's unique time management system. He uses just a few techniques which put goals up front and in harmony with his current responsibilities. His parents were goal oriented, and John modeled his organization after theirs. As a youngster, he was encouraged to set short-term goals in sports and studies. A high school teacher and one college coach also advised him on the elements of successful time management, describing the techniques they valued. John listened and made some modifications to suit his personality. John's own time management system is based on goals he sets for himself and which he regularly reviews. These goals touch on what he wants to establish and to maintain in his personal and professional life.

Personal Goals: "I've watched too many high school and college coaches who are married to their sports with no time for family, relaxation, and enjoyment," John points out. "That's not for me. My profession is important, but so is the rest of my life." Because of these beliefs, John examined some personal goals with his wife. Together, they determined the following:

- In what kind and size community they wanted to live (a small college town).
- In what part of the country (close to both of their parents and to the skiing they both love).
- The lifestyle both wanted and the income necessary to maintain it (his wife is now working half-time).
- The time they were willing to spend working on personal development, on community projects, socializing and relaxing.

John and his wife discussed their goals and made decisions based on their preferences. While both could easily be overwhelmed by activities and commitments, they take time to review their personal goals as part of each week's routine.

"It is easy to add more. Our friends and associates regularly ask us to chair a committee or help out in some way," John reports. "Our time is limited, and there are certain essentials we both want. Saying no to requests beyond our limits is easier with these goals. We feel less guilt because the decision is related to our family plan, and is not a hastily made choice which we would regret later."

Professional Goals: John defined his professional goals to be consistent with his personal ones. He very carefully determined what was necessary to become a successful coach. He saw that he had to build a sound program in each coaching assignment and to help young people develop. With these two goals in mind, John was determined to do his best.

But John also had his eye on a position and setting where he would like to spend the majority of his coaching years. Through a long process of constant self-evaluation, John determined that a medium-sized university was the best place for him. Furthermore, of all the sports he had coached, he found track the most enjoyable. He then discussed his decision with the people who knew him best and sought advice from past coaches on the directions he ought to pursue. They reinforced his decision to pursue a position coaching track that also had administrative responsibilities.

ESTABLISHING A TIME LINE

John also went a step further. Through conversations with his wife and close friends, he established a rough time line for becoming a head track coach and athletic director. "Put the emphasis on rough," John adds. "But I do keep that goal in mind and take steps each day to reach it. Sometimes the steps are small, sometimes they're major."

John's yearly, 6-month and 3-month plans reveal his determination to advance. John believes that without them the pressure of his immediate responsibilities might eliminate any thoughts about the future. He feels opportunities spring from these plans, and so relies on his own planning rather than luck.

John believes these plans give him time to grow and to become more capable. At the end of each year, he looks back on his professional accomplishments and then identifies the next 12 months' targets. He honestly evaluates his coaching and administrative abilities at this time and determines where he needs to improve. He then determines which realistic activities will produce the changes he desires. Usually, those activities include a combination of organized reading, a few carefully selected seminars, and conversations with more experienced coaches. In addition, 2 years ago, he enrolled in a master's program in business administration.

With the year charted, John can look ahead 6 months and then work back to what will happen in 3-month blocks of time. "I have my eye on accomplishments over the short term," he says. "They boost my enthusiasm to continue." John gets even more specific, translating his goals into plans weekly. By doing this, he constantly reminds himself of progress to be made and of accomplishments already achieved. His progress evaluation is ongoing, and he shares the results with his wife, associates, and friends.

How much time does all this planning take? According to John, less than an hour each week. He has developed the habit of regularly looking back as the basis for projecting ahead. On a Friday afternoon, John looks back at the week's accomplishments and begins to sketch out his plan for the week to come. Then on Monday morning, he takes about 10 minutes to identify his major targets for the week.

John's Weekly Plan: John recognizes that a variety of demands are made upon his limited time and is aware that he must fulfill his current professional responsibilities. "Building an athletic program and working with young athletes is time-consuming and emotionally demanding," he emphasizes. "It could drain away every hour in the day and leave me too exhausted for family and my lifetime ambitions. My weekly plan is the harness which keeps me from digressing too much. Some things will take me away from that plan, but I always come back to it."

Making and relying on that weekly plan is a habit with John. At the end of each week, he reviews what he has accomplished and then looks ahead to the next. He identifies relatively few major responsibilities and tasks he must finish that week, as well as tasks he must at least start. This weekly plan also takes into account his personal growth targets and his family-related activities.

John shares his plan with the key people with whom he works: the athletic director, the athletic department secretary, and the part-time assistant coach who is available 3 days a week. John and his wife share their weekly plans, being sure to cut back on their busy schedules for relaxation time. By sharing his weekly plans with the important people in his life, John can get feedback on anything he might have omitted, as well as keep everyone informed as to his intentions. "It takes very little time, reduces surprises for them, and keeps me from forgetting," John says.

JOHN'S ORGANIZATIONAL SYSTEM

One of John's organizing techniques is to have different-colored folders for major activities. He has found that this enables him to file his papers correctly and to find the right file when he needs it. He throws out those papers not fitting into his categories.

This filing system also involves another organizing technique: evaluating papers of all kinds and deciding what he should keep. He throws out items for which he cannot find a use now or for which he cannot anticipate a use. John estimates that he immediately throws out at least 40% of all the letters, mass mail, and assorted announcements he gets. This leaves less to clutter his desk, office, and mind.

"I find what I need more easily by organizing paper each day, instead of letting it pile up," John reports. The folders are an effective organizing tool for him and are labeled as follows:

- Practice Plans
- Competition
- Recruiting
- Department Responsibilities
- Personal
- Other

He keeps these files on his desk and available for regular use with additional folders in a nearby cabinet. His filing system is a bit more elaborate. There are files for individual meets, athletes, and some major department responsibilities, such as committees and reports he must prepare. But John has vowed to use only one filing cabinet because he believes more space usually leads to additional unnecessary clutter.

Plans and paper organization which reinforce his clearly defined sense of direction are two important parts of his time management program. But John also pays attention to a climate that increases his productivity. He knows certain athletes, students, and colleagues have a rightful claim to some of his time: He realizes that their habit of dropping by all the time could limit his ability to concentrate on one task at a time. Therefore, John looks for some simple ways to keep his mind from wandering.

SELF-DISCIPLINE

A few mental reminders help John keep on track. He uses three that a friend suggested and which he molded to suit his style.

1. *Whoa* is his reminder to stop, think, and ask, "What should I be doing right now?" This one word forces his attention back to his weekly plan and tends to emphasize the need to do the most important work first. When many people make demands simultaneously, John thinks of his reminder word to help him control frantic and purposeless movement.

2. *PF* stands for past and future and helps John to slow down, look back, and then ahead. In the midst of busy and interruption-prone days, John plans for intelligent use of the limited amounts of time available to him. He organizes the minutes between appointments and meetings for limited, but beneficial accomplishments.

3. *Target* reminds John to ask himself, "Am I on target and dealing with high priorities first?" It helps John determine if a request is really important and enables him to control tempting distractions

"These reminders slow me down and are my personal distress-control method," John says. "They stop me from running off in too many directions."

These words keep John from climbing up the stress continuum. He has seen too many coaches allow events and other people to run their lives. Although John takes pride in being successful, he does not want to let his surroundings become unnecessarily frantic. These three words, along with his belief in his ability to manage each day, help John keep stress from reaching destructive levels.

These few techniques are John's personal recipe for time management. He is convinced they are enough to help him reach the goals he considers important. Although he has experimented with other methods, he finds he keeps returning to the same ones he has formed from habit.

You need not emulate John exactly, but you can examine his approach and learn from his experience and success. Selecting and adapting a recipe to suit your own style and personality is better than copying one you do not like.

The eight techniques John uses are listed below. Before you go on to chapter 6, take a minute to review these techniques and determine which, if any, you would like to consider as part of your own recipe.

JOHN GIBBS' RECIPE FOR SUCCESS

1. Establish yearly, 6-month, and 3-month goals and monitor them regularly.
2. Develop a timetable for achieving certain major accomplishments and milestones to measure progress.
3. Ensure consistency between personal goals and coaching goals.
4. Plan for each week, emphasizing high-priority work.
5. Communicate plans to key colleagues to avoid leaving out necessary activities and receive feedback.
6. Organize a filing system built on important activities.
7. Throw out irrelevant paper.
8. Use self-disciplining cues to slow down, to focus on the important, and to control the stress level.

Chapter 6
Planning for a Complex Life

1
Time Management and Sports
a. Ineffective time management
b. The ACORN environment

2
Analyzing Time Use
a. Self-evaluation and self-monitoring
b. Personal time management recipes

3
Establishing Direction
a. Setting goals, priorities, and limits
b. Detail management

4
Maintaining Control
a. Active concentration
b. Stress—and distress management

5-9
Time Management Techniques in Practice
Goal Setting (Chap. 5)
Routine Planning (Chap. 6)
Task Orienting (Chap. 7)
Demand Control (Chap. 8)
Limit Maintenance (Chap. 9)

10
Starting and Maintaining Effective Time Management
a. Selecting and using techniques
b. Reaching out to others

PRIORITIZING GOALS: ANN DAVIS

Ann Davis enjoys her job coaching girls' high school basketball, but that is only part of her busy and full life. "I'm what you would call a restless educator," she admits. "A lot of projects going on at the same time makes each day exciting." Her busy days begin very early. Ann, her husband, and her children take care of their family responsibilities before leaving the house. The Davis family has a simple but effective plan that is the foundation for their morning and evening routine. Each of their duties is listed, including who prepares breakfast and cleans up afterward. "I think the whole family is more comfortable with this plan," Ann believes. "Before we put it together, my husband and children tended to rely on me alone to keep the house in order."

Ann has been a planner all her life. "My parents always worked and were active in our community. Our family plan kept all five of us from going in too many directions at once and from forgetting our important responsibilities." Involvement also was part of Ann's life. "You get back as much as you put into life," her parents regularly advised. Thus, Ann found time to be on school committees and sports teams in high school and college, in addition to maintaining a solid "B" average.

Living things have been a fascination for Ann since she was barely old enough to hold a frog. "Biology was just my natural major and teaching was a passion," she asserts. "It's wonderful watching high school students get excited about science." Her professional association is becoming another kind of passion. "Teachers have to act more independently," Ann believes. "Our association is a means, a legitimate means, to make our interests known." It is obvious from her comments that Ann feels deeply about the association. She has held an assortment of committee chairs and offices. "Never vice president or president," Ann maintains. "Then the association would become my whole life, and there are too many other things that are important to me."

Basketball is one of them, playing it with her brothers and on girls' high school and college teams. "I still scrimmage with the players because the game is so much fun," she says. Her teams do win, but that seems secondary to the fun the players and Ann seem to be having in practice and at games. "Basketball is enjoyable to all of us because we learn and improve," Ann adds. "We don't have the time or inclination to allow the players to goof around. They are all busy people and appreciate the discipline."

Family also is central to Ann's life. "Why have a family if you don't take time to be a part of it," she reminds herself when she is overloaded with requests. "That is when my 'no' is very emphatic." As a mother, Ann does her share of volunteering in the children's school. Occasionally, she collects for a few charitable drives.

"I'm always conscious of overcommitment. My inclination is to say 'yes' or 'I'll get to it', which is really the same as 'yes.' Ever since a bout with exhaustion 5 years ago, I've learned to control that 'yes' tendency. Now I want to do just a few things well. What they are is pretty clear to me and to those in my life."

For Ann, those few things are family, teaching, coaching, and the professional association. Ann has always sought excellence, put forth the extra effort needed to obtain it and, in fact, plans for it. In doing so, she uses a few time management techniques to buttress those plans.

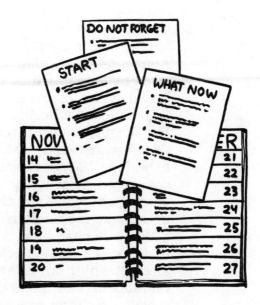

ROUTINE PLANNING

Ann has the following three planning activities to bring organization to each of her very busy and sometimes tense weeks:

1. Weekly plan
2. Don't Forget list
3. What Now list

Like John Gibbs, Ann sketches out what she would like to accomplish each week in her four major responsibilities. "I try to identify what must be done that week or at least started," she says. "Procrastination has always been a problem for me. Keeping the important out front and visible, lessens the temptation to put things off." Although some work won't be due for a week or more, I go ahead and start it. I feel better when deadline pressure is reduced," she adds. On her weekly plan is a special column labeled, "Start," under which two or three projects are listed. Each of these projects is broken into segments to encourage starting one piece in the time that becomes available.

Ann carries around her weekly plan in a loose-leaf binder that has sections for each of her classes and coaching work. The binder and her yearly calendar are with her all the time. "They reinforce each other and help me stay within realistic limits," she claims. For emphasis, she prepares another list to organize her busy life.

Ann's Don't Forget list is clipped to the top of her calendar. She makes it each morning just before breakfast, usually in consultation with her husband and children, who also make similar lists and carry them around as reminders. With this list, she usually manages to complete necessary tasks, make important phone calls, and attend necessary meetings. As a result, she has fewer crises caused by forgetfulness. Because Ann is constantly on the run, she keeps the list with her. It would be useless on her desk calendar because she spends so little time in the office. "A U.S. Senator used a list like that," Ann reports. "My high school class visited his office. We were awed by how much he did in a day. He mentioned the list. It seemed so logical then and is a habit now."

One more list helps Ann to concentrate and to slow down: Her What Now list exerts a calming influence and minimizes the pressure caused by a constant awareness of what remains to be done. "My days are really chopped up between classes, coaching, and everything else," Ann says. "I'm an excitable person, and what remains to be done could and sometimes does make me nervous."

When she had time, Ann used to waste it wondering what to do, or she would decide she did not have enough time to attempt anything of value and instead would spend 15 minutes or half an hour socializing. "It was half-hearted socializing," Ann recalls. "My attention was on all the work I had to do. But 15 minutes never seemed enough time to do anything worthwhile."

A friend in the insurance business showed Ann a trick she'd learned from an experienced supervisor. "It's nothing more than slowing down to set some immediate priorities," this friend told Ann. "Instead of running around trying to figure out what to do or deciding to waste time, take a moment to plan." The idea of a moment to plan appealed to Ann. In her short periods of time, she thought about what she could accomplish during the day. From this emerged her What Now list. Depending on the amount of time available, she now works on parts of major assignments or completes routine tasks.

"My determination increases with those lists. Maybe I challenge myself to get more done. It is certainly easier to concentrate when I know my direction," she emphasizes.

LEARNING TO COMPLETE A TASK QUICKLY

These short lists have made Ann aware of completion speed. "When I do a portion of a major task, the time it takes tells me about how long the rest will require," she asserts. "It's usually more than I anticipated. This warns me to start earlier on what's left to hold down last-minute deadline pressure." Her desire to hold down pressure also led to another technique for keeping the routine from overpowering her and her priorities. Ann learned the value of doing routine rapidly and now values this habit for its results.

When Ann began teaching, she was overwhelmed by the amount of paperwork. "How do you every get through it all?" she asked a more experienced colleague. "I don't!" was the response. Ann found that her colleague ignored 70% of it and set aside the remaining 30% for review at some other time, usually when she was too tired to do anything important.

Because her colleague believed that 70% didn't deserve her attention, she felt the chances of any problems arising from not reviewing it were slim. "If something is important enough to produce a follow-up letter or call, you will know a response is necessary," the teacher told Ann.

Ann was not entirely comfortable with that approach to paperwork. However, she did like the idea of doing routine and often low-priority work at one time. So, she developed rapid routines for doing routine work. When possible, Ann fills out forms at one time, records grades, makes phone calls, and orders supplies. "I seem to do them more quickly as a group," she believes.

As she gained experience and confidence, Ann became more willing to tear up a request or throw out an informational item before reading it in depth. "The title tells me if it deserves attention or not," she says. Ann is equally concerned about reducing the impact that interruptions can have on each day. Again, her approach is an honest one.

CONTROLLING INTER-RUPTIONS

Ann learned how to control interruptions from another colleague. At first, she found it difficult to ask a student or player to come back later. "I told a colleague that I was a teacher and a coach, not to mention mother and association leader," she recalls. "Those are service roles. When people need me, I have to be available." That was an early rationalization. Her comment, made in the teacher's lounge, was a response to a colleague who described all the ways he kept people away. Ann was irritated at his attitude and said so. After the exchange, a colleague she respected, and also a part-time coach, took Ann aside to point out a kernel of value in the "avoider's" remarks.

This colleague advised Ann that although she should not shut people out, she should not let everyone have a claim on her time. She urged Ann to use some kind of control, perhaps by diplomatically asking a visitor the purpose of the visit.

Ann's friend had found this directed the visitor directly to the problem.

Ann liked this teacher's honesty and the simplicity of the approaches she used. At a time management seminar for teachers, she had heard several gimmicks to control interruptions, including removing chairs near the desk, never sitting down when someone drops in, looking at the clock, and lying about an impending meeting. These techniques struck Ann as dishonest and likely to lead to poor relationships. For Ann, honesty has worked. She now finds it easy to ask people to come back later, usually explaining why she cannot talk at that time. Although she takes time for necessary interruptions, she finds she now has more control over them.

PREVENTING PROCRASTINATION

Another group of techniques keep Ann from relying on mythical time. Because she dislikes pressure, she has devised some mental cues which increase her willingness to start a task right away rather than to rationalize why it can be put off for another time.

Reminder phrases have become part of Ann's mental baggage; they are very similar to John Gibbs' mental-disciplining devices. She uses them whenever her tendencies to procrastinate emerge.

1. *Manageable units* tells Ann to break larger tasks into smaller ones that can be done in shorter periods of time.

2. *Opportunity for excellence* suggests that if Ann starts a task sooner, she will have a chance to review her work before it is due and make the final product that much better.

3. *Not worth a whimper* reminds Ann to get the seemingly unpleasant household chores done without think-

ing about them or complaining. "It takes more energy to complain than do them," she laughs.

4. *Effect on others* points out that procrastination affects friends, colleagues, and students. When Ann's work is late, these people are under more pressure. Ann is especially aware that time is a collective resource. Because she dislikes pressure so much herself, she is sensitive to reducing it for others.

REACHING AN ORGANIZATIONAL PLATEAU

Ann's final time management technique is more of an attitude than an organizing habit. Her technique is to pat herself on the back each day by reviewing what she has accomplished. That review shows Ann her unique time management recipe is working: She is completing what has to be done and maintaining the balance she needs.

"I'm as organized as I want to be," she points out. For Ann, planning, doing routine items fast, controlling interruptions, and confronting procrastination are a means to a desired end; they are all she needs. With these few habits, Ann is able to meet her coaching, teaching, association, and family responsibilities.

Do any of the techniques Ann uses appeal to you? Here is Ann Davis' recipe for successful time management.

ANN DAVIS' RECIPE FOR SUCCESS

1. Identify a few central responsibilities and make a commitment to give them primary attention.
2. Plan for a week at a time and use that plan to identify a few projects that can be started early.
3. Prepare a reminder list of necessary details and keep the list with you at all times.
4. Plan to get the routine tasks out of the way in short periods of time.
5. Evaluate how long it takes to complete important projects so enough time can be allotted.
6. Develop routines to get the routine done fast and consider if any of it can be eliminated.
7. Control interruptions honestly by making others aware of your need for privacy.
8. Prevent procrastination with mental disciplining cues.
9. Pat yourself on the back each day by reviewing accomplishments.

Chapter 7
Staying on Task

1
Time Management and Sports
a. Ineffective time management
b. The ACORN environment

2
Analyzing Time Use
a. Self-evaluation and self-monitoring
b. Personal time management recipes

3
Establishing Direction
a. Setting goals, priorities, and limits
b. Detail management

4
Maintaining Control
a. Active concentration
b. Stress—and distress management

5-9
Time Management Techniques in Practice
Goal Setting (Chap. 5)
Routine Planning (Chap. 6)
Task Orienting (Chap. 7)
Demand Control (Chap. 8)
Limit Maintenance (Chap. 9)

10
Starting and Maintaining Effective Time Management
a. Selecting and using techniques
b. Reaching out to others

ORGANIZING SUCCESSFULLY: KEN RAPPEL

"If I hadn't been born and raised in Minnesota, life really wouldn't have been worth living," Ken Rappel often comments. It is his love of skiing that prompts this dramatic statement. Although Ken enjoys other sports and finds pleasure in the brief summers, he looks forward to the return of the ski season.

Ken admits he is addicted to downhill skiing. "Not quite Olympic caliber" is how he honestly evaluates his abilities, but he has enough trophies and ribbons to demonstrate he is better than many. He even tried competition for one season after graduating from college. "That was enough; I went back to get an MBA," Ken reports.

Master's in Business Administration in hand, Ken found a management position with a Minneapolis-based corporation. "Business was similar to summer—enjoyable, but not really engaging," Ken recalls. "I didn't look forward to each day with the same enthusiasm as skiing." So he took a risk and became the full-time director of a ski club. Ken now runs several teams, including one that competes in regional and national meets. He also has instructional programs and an equipment shop to manage as well. For the present, Ken is the sole employee. If business increases, however, he may be able to hire additional personnel. "I really have the best of two worlds, skiing and business," Ken says with enthusiasm. "Maybe the worst on bad days. Life is certainly exciting and very full."

Although he was not trained to coach, Ken found pleasure in helping young people develop and older ones overcome limited self-confidence. "I was surprised at my patience," he reports. "Encouraging others to learn is almost as much fun as competing."

Although Ken's club is only a few years old, its popularity has grown. Classes are full and clothing and equipment sales are steady. His coaching ability and business sense are a potent combination. Ken very much wants to see the club grow. His competitive and managerial experience have a decided effect on how he approaches what must be done to become successful and stay that way.

Ken was not always such a successful organizer. He did well enough in high school and college to be admitted to an MBA program as a trial student. To help him get through the program, Ken joined a study group of students from his part of the city, two of whom were "super-organized." They suggested a few time management techniques which would enable him to keep up with studies and still be able to ski.

Ken's personal recipe for time management emerged through experimentation and some difficult changes in his approach to life. "My old tendencies are still there," Ken admits. "I can still waste time on dozens of diversions, lose details in the process, and fail to keep on top of all things. But each day I feel a little more disciplined and less likely to fritter away my energy." Ken was able to draw on certain disciplining skills competitive skiing had instilled. His desire to succeed is an important motivator now, and he has found work truly enjoyable. Coaching brings him pleasure, as does an expanding club now beginning to make money. Time management is helping Ken achieve goals that produce regular satisfaction.

TASK ORIENTING

Concentrating on one task at a time is the foundation for Ken's approach to self-organization. He generally works back from the outcome and due date to the beginning point of each major project. From that mental picture, Ken outlines all the activities or steps to be completed. He makes lists of what must be done each day and plots out the major tasks in his mind from start to finish.

"This method is a combination of how my coach told me to prepare for an event and the long-range planning that one of my MBA instructors described," Ken says. In both cases, the outcome becomes the motivator, and what must be done along the way is clear from the start.

"There are some additional benefits to this mental planning," Ken reports. "Knowing the outcome desired and the steps to reach it encourages me to start sooner and to stay with an important task to completion, in spite of many interruptions." Instead of starting a new activity, Ken is likely to return to the original one and begin where he left off. This mental discipline reduces the impact of the interruptions which seem to occur every few minutes.

"You can't get ahead of yourself in skiing or business," he maintains. "With concentration, a downhill run or a budget will turn out well. Both need undivided attention from start to finish."

CONTROLLING INTERRUPTIONS

"Enthusiasm can be dangerous," Ken believes. "I can get excited about all the opportunities and wind up going in several directions at one time. Sometimes it is just a case of daydreaming when I should be doing something more constructive. Whatever the reason, valuable time disappears and I wind up with too much left to do at the end of the day. Focusing on one task at a time helps me control the wandering my enthusiasm can produce." As an educational businessman, Ken is constantly interrupted. Multiple demands on his time are common. Because of this, it would be easy for him to put aside planning group practices, preparing for away competitions, inventory taking of stock, or paying bills in favor of answering interesting questions from a student or taking time for an unannounced salesperson's visit.

"I am more likely to postpone answering the question or taking time for the salesperson when I concentrate on finishing a task," Ken observes. "Obviously some interruptions cannot wait, but I find I listen better after finishing an important job."

Even when he is interrupted for an hour or more, Ken returns to a major assignment. The closer he gets to finishing, the more he is determined to complete the remaining steps. At this point, Ken "locks into" his work and cannot stop even if he tries.

PREVENTING SELF-INTERRUPTION

A combination of suggestions from a former coach and a fellow student showed Ken how he could stop interrupting himself.

The coach told Ken to commit to an excellent performance before starting, with a simple self-directing message: "Keep low all the way" was one such message. "It will build your determination," the coach advised. Within the limits of Ken's skiing ability, those messages did inspire better runs.

Now he uses a "Before I stop" direction to himself as a way to prevent self-interruption. For example, he says to himself, "Before I stop, I'll have planned the team's next practice," or "Before I stop, I'll have finished the monthly order." This method encourages Ken to spend more time on finishing a single task.

What Ken learned from his fellow student was purely through observation. This student worked in a somewhat stark room, free of distractions. Her desk was not cluttered with extra paper and books, and she kept what she needed within arm's reach to reduce the amount of time spent jumping up and down. She also kept her telephone within an arm's reach but out of her line of vision. Her room had adequate lighting, and her chair was comfortable enough to prevent squirming, but not too soft to encourage napping.

Ken contrasted her businesslike setting with the chaos of his own study area. He had papers stacked everywhere, with "get to's" mixed in with important material. When Ken started working, he thought about that student and contrasted her approach to his own disorganized, cluttered methods. He decided to make few changes to his own style. He put his phone on his left side where it was easy to reach but not a distraction. He put his "get to" pile on a bookshelf and skimmed all the material first. With this approach, Ken found that at least 50% of the paper could be tossed away immediately. He put major tasks in separate folders so that the paper and forms belonging together stayed that way. Finally, he arranged pictures and other clutter so they were not a constant presence and perpetual distractor.

Paper still accumulates in Ken's office, but his commitment to succeed makes his small office less of a storage area and more of a workplace. Furthermore, being able to find important papers faster is something he values. In a less cluttered office, he is able to keep himself self-directed, not self-interrupted.

REGULAR SELF-EVALUATION

To prevent himself from slipping back into old ways, Ken regularly self-evaluates. This helps emphasize the benefits time management is producing and also builds and maintains his motivation.

Once in the morning, once in the midafternoon, and just before the regular day ends, Ken slows down to look at his activities and accomplishments. "This is the time when I talk to myself; it's a one-man operation," he points out. Ken first identifies what he has done and looks at how self-organization contributed to that success. Self-criticism comes next with the emphasis on logical and necessary improvements in planning and execution.

How and why did evaluation become a time management technique? Again his former coach and fellow-students had an influence. The coach told him to assess his accomplishments and activities during and at the end of each practice. "We worked alone a great deal; our coach suggested that this would help us develop self-discipline," Ken said. "Without it, one flop could make us feel we'd never improve."

His fellow-students used self-evaluation to test how much of the assigned material they had mastered. "They called this brief review and self-examination a confidence booster," Ken adds. "Your motivation to go on usually increases when you can see the progress you've made." This technique keeps Ken's enthusiasm high and his discipline intact. "Not all the time," Ken admits, "but more than in the past. I wish someone had told me to self-evaluate about 10 years ago when I was in college!"

MANAGING IMPORTANT DETAILS

"Those who don't study the past are cursed to repeat it": Ken had heard this proverb on many occasions. He learned the relevance of the principle during his MBA program. In one class, he was required to gather and to analyze details from past crises. The professors explained how several businesses had successfully used this data-gathering process to prevent future problems.

A visiting attorney once explained that details were often essential for legal action. If an injured employee sued an employer, the manager in charge at the time of the incident would have to report what happened. Liability for negligence often depended on the manager's ability to remember the details.

Ken knew that negligence could mean lost money. He also realized that details captured for reuse would cut down the amount of time needed for planning and organizing. When Ken started directing the club, he discovered how useful it was to collect names and phone numbers of key equipment suppliers, record transportation costs and travel times to competition sites, and keep a written record of other important details.

"In a one-person business, my time is an important part of the inventory," Ken asserts. He keeps details on team and individual practices, meet organizing steps, and a number of business procedures he follows. He keeps them all in separate folders and habitually checks for guidance and for updating procedures. The files are a guide on which he relies each day.

"My memory is in writing," Ken emphasizes. "No more looking around for old forms or calling friends who are more organized. I don't feel as pressured because I know where I can find important records quickly."

SETTING AND KEEPING DEADLINES

"I will never use 'as soon as possible' again," Ken says emphatically. "You can't run anything on the hope that you'll have work done when you need it. Deadlines and due dates have to be set."

In addition to erasing that phrase from his vocabulary, Ken now lists what he expects others to do and when. That regularly made and reviewed list contains names of team members, parents helping out with club teams, equipment suppliers, and ski associations. Each day, Ken notes on a pad near his phone whom he needs to remind.

"Some people need to be pushed a little, others a lot," Ken points out. "But none of these calls take very long, and most of the time, the work gets done on time. I just have to pick up the slack."

Specific dates and diplomatic reminders are essential to making this technique work. What's more, most of the people on his list expect Ken's reminders and appreciate them.

Ken is happy about his success in what he calls an educational business. "I enjoy making all the pieces come together," he says. "Teaching others to ski is almost as much fun as skiing." For Ken, organization and time management are only a means to an end. It's the achievements, young people and adults skiing well, competitive teams, and a business making money that are so important to him.

Does Ken's recipe appeal to you? Listed below are the ingredients of Ken Rappel's formula for successful time management.

KEN RAPPEL'S RECIPE FOR SUCCESS

1. Focus on one task at a time.
2. Mentally establish successful outcomes for one task and work back to identify the details that lead there.
3. Organize a work area to be comfortable but distraction-free.
4. Do not self-interrupt; lock in with self-directing messages.
5. Self-monitor regularly to review accomplishments for an established period of time and use the review to encourage self-direction.
6. Capture important details in writing and develop reminder files with the details of regularly used procedures.
7. Set and keep deadlines for yourself and others, using reminders for individuals who tend to be late.

Chapter 8
Sorting Out the Demands

1
Time Management and Sports
a. Ineffective time management
b. The ACORN environment

2
Analyzing Time Use
a. Self-evaluation and self-monitoring
b. Personal time management recipes

3
Establishing Direction
a. Setting goals, priorities, and limits
b. Detail management

4
Maintaining Control
a. Active concentration
b. Stress—and distress management

5-9
Time Management Techniques in Practice
Goal Setting (Chap. 5)
Routine Planning (Chap. 6)
Task Orienting (Chap. 7)
Demand Control (Chap. 8)
Limit Maintenance (Chap. 9)

10
Starting and Maintaining Effective Time Management
a. Selecting and using techniques
b. Reaching out to others

MANAGING TIME AND DEMANDS: SANDRA GRUETTER

Sandra Gruetter was greatly influenced early in life by a negative example—her father. All her adult life, she has thought about what a lack of priorities did to him. Now as coach and teacher, Sandra tries to avoid the schedule which prematurely ended her father's life.

Ed Gruetter was a well-meaning person who collapsed from a heart attack when Sandra was a senior in high school. As a plant superintendent, he claimed his days were occupied by one crisis after another. "I watched the pressure kill him, even though we urged him to slow down," Sandra says sadly.

"He had no routine. Even at home, Dad would drop everything if a friend called for help. Her father usually went to work early, skipped lunch, and stayed late to catch up on unfinished paperwork. "He complained that helping so many other people made it virtually impossible for him to finish his own work during the day," Sandra recalls.

Nevertheless, he was always available and ready to help. Sometimes he would even volunteer for extra work, fearing no one else would step in to pick up the slack. "'Can't you say no?' we used to ask him," Sandra remembers. "But even though he said he tried, he never knew how."

After her father's death, Sandra realized she had the same tendency to never say no. It just seemed natural to always volunteer, and because others knew this, she was constantly called on for assistance. Her father's death shocked her into acknowledging the consequences of such behavior. She vowed to avoid the lifestyle which contributed to his early death. So Sandra began to look for people who unlike her father were able to manage time and the demands made on them.

DEMAND CONTROL

Sandra began to study her high school teachers and coaches and found that many had an ability to *control demands*. As both educators and people with family and personal responsibilities, they were very clear about what was and was not important. "I was really surprised at their determination to control demands on their time," Sandra recalls. The possibility of controlling demands without suffering negative consequences amazed her. She learned that people are more in charge of events in their lives than they often imagine.

The second time management habit Sandra noticed was that these same busy people also found time to get away, think, plan, or just relax. "And nothing happened when they did," Sandra adds. "With just those two techniques, they controlled each day to a far greater extent than my father felt was possible. And look what they get done!" She went on to describe how these teachers and coaches handled a variety of responsibilities and had a life apart from their professional careers.

In college, Sandra began to experiment with controlling demands and finding time for herself. She backed off from all the commitments she used to make, and tried to let her own needs influence her more than other peoples' agendas. Gradually, she became more comfortable with these two time management techniques. She chose intercollegiate athletics, an English education major, and physical education minor as her three major activities and began to ignore many other minor distractions.

"I always was afraid of the consequences. I worried about what people would think of me if I said no to a request," Sandra reported. "Most didn't react negatively and there was less pressure on me."

Although Sandra found it relatively easy to use control in college, her new-found habits were sorely tempted when she began coaching and teaching. The number of challenging activities seem unlimited, and she was troubled about not doing enough for the students and athletes. Because Sandra coached two sports at a preparatory school, cross-country/track and swimming, in addition to being women's athletic director and an English teacher, she had to develop high, middle, and low priorities in each area of responsibility. Sandra is extremely capable, but is saddled with a willingness to take on more than she can handle.

"But I'm on the alert," Sandra points out emphatically. Her father's death constantly reminds her to slow down too-ready acceptance of just one more task. While she hasn't abandoned her service orientation entirely, Sandra also wants to enjoy life and to reduce the pressure that unrelenting demands can put upon her. Time management will help her reach these goals. Sandra's unique program centers on controlling demands and finding time to pull back for thought, planning, and relaxation.

SLOWING DOWN FOR SUCCESS

"Continuing demand analysis" is at the center of Sandra's time management program. "It's not as fancy as it sounds," she hastens to point out. "All I do is analyze what I could do versus what I must do."

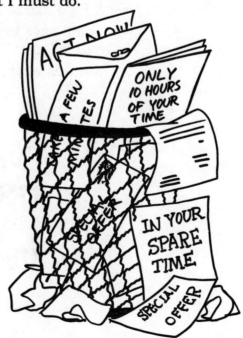

She learned much of her approach from a time management film shown at a coaching clinic. In the film, a busy and pressured executive was taught how to sort papers into stacks according to their level of importance. This method involved pushing the low-priority material to last place or discarding it entirely.

Sandra adapted this method by putting low-priority work out of sight. "I use two drawers, one in my office at school and the other in my desk at home," she says. "I ask myself: Can this wait? If the answer is yes, in it goes!" As she is asking herself this question, she can evaluate the value of the paper altogether. In fact, Sandra finds that she throws out about 80% of it. That one step alone reduces the pressure on her. So far, she reports, there have been no repercussions from throwing out so much material.

DISTINGUISHING THE REALLY URGENT FROM THE SEEMINGLY URGENT

Blowing a whistle on the urgent is Sandra's second time management technique. She learned this one from her college advisor. "What seems urgent to you, or more likely to someone else will constantly try to displace what really counts. You could run in a dozen different directions at once and end up doing nothing!" she warned Sandra.

Everytime something "urgent" comes up, Sandra tells herself to "wait a minute." Those three words allow her to stop and look at what she is able to do and to decide if she should in fact do it. She gives herself a few moments to look at her primary responsibilities and to make a decision. Also she uses phrases her father never did.

- "No, I'd like to help out, but it just isn't possible."
- "You'll have to work it out yourself now; I just don't have time today."
- "Not this week, maybe next."

"Of course, I don't say no all the time," she emphasizes. "But my time is limited and if I'm not careful, my days, evenings, and weekends would be in other people's hands."

Sandra discovered that this method has positive consequences. She finds that people respect her time, and she receives fewer silly requests. Consequently, she has more time for herself, and for her athletes.

FINDING TIME FOR PERSONAL NEEDS

A coach Sandra respected once shared with her a valuable time management technique. This coach advised her that it is impossible to think on the run or when pulled in several directions at once. He emphasized that time for thinking, planning, and relaxing was a crucial part of each day and told Sandra about the three periods each day he took out from his busy schedule:

- Before he left the house, he mentally visualized the day, jotted some reminder notes, and prepared himself for a busy schedule.
- At midday during the season, he reviewed practice plans—off-season, he would relax with a swim, a walk on campus, or lunch with friends.
- Early in the evening, he left at least 30 minutes free for relaxation or activities not related to coaching.

Because Sandra is not much of a morning person, she found that the first period did not work for her. But the other two were appealing and became a fixture in her daily routine. "They both are invaluable but for different reasons," Sandra reports. "An hour to think at noon or get away is my control mechanism. During the season, I spend it working on practices, fine-tuning the details." Off-season, she uses the hour for herself. Once or twice a week, Sandra and a few teachers get away for lunch, and she often finds a quiet spot just to read a book. Her evening slowdown is a 7-day-a-week, year-round habit. "I always find time for this. Sometimes I just sit. In good weather, I might take a walk or a bike ride," Sandra says.

GETTING TO THE POINT

Sandra also found that she was pressured by calls which seemed to go on forever. When she saw an article in a popular magazine on how much time executives waste on the phone, she was immediately interested. "Half the time I lost interest or couldn't figure out what the caller wanted," Sandra complained.

As a coach, Sandra has to get and give a great deal of information, and most of the calls have to be sandwiched into a busy daily schedule. From the article, Sandra learned how to treat a call as a short-targeted meeting and reduce the time each requires. She particularly liked setting an agenda at the start of a call with direction-setting phrases such as,

- "I have four items to discuss with you."
- "Is this a good time for us to talk?"
- "Is there anything else we need to discuss now?"

She was amazed at how well-accepted direction setting was. "It was as if the people I called appreciated this organization," Sandra commented. She found that keeping callers on track was more difficult, but by asking, "How can I help you?" Sandra was able to guide most callers to the point. "Most people didn't take offense and seemed pleased at being able to end a conversation quickly with results," she said.

Because Sandra found that direction setting was particularly successful for telephone calls, she began to use the same approach in face-to-face meetings. "I want to find time for colleagues and especially players," she emphasizes. "But some people seem to go on and on with no point in their conversation."

Slowly and carefully, Sandra introduced the same sort of phrases in meetings:

- "What do we need to discuss now?"
- "If I understand what you are suggesting..."
- "You would like me to do what?"
- "Is there anything else we need to discuss now?"

Although some of Sandra's colleagues joke about Sandra's efficiency, she notices that players who come to talk get to the point sooner. Team meetings, when they are held, move along purposefully. Sandra announces the agenda and stays with it. Again, she believes players and assistant coaches listen more.

RESPONSE EFFICIENCY

Sandra's final technique came from an interview she read in a local paper in which an executive discussed how she had cut down on the number of secretaries her firm needed. This executive found it was easier and less expensive to simply write or to personally type a response on the bottom of the letters she received.

Sandra was a little nervous to try the same technique, but it appealed to her so she tried it anyway. Reactions were positive or at least noncommittal. She found that she did paperwork faster by handwriting a response and that she could say what she needed to in a note, rather than a lengthy, typewritten letter. She also began making short telephone calls instead of writing a memo whenever possible.

These few techniques bring Sandra a level of control she values a great deal. They enable her to hold down demands, to feel less pressure, and to contribute more as a coach and teacher. She still sometimes finds herself tempted to take on more and to treat every activity as a high priority, but by sorting out demands, controlling them, and finding time for herself, Sandra is better able to discern important activities from those that intrude on her already pressured life. Here is Sandra Gruetter's recipe for successful time management:

SANDRA GRUETTER'S RECIPE FOR SUCCESS

1. Concentrate on controlling demands and finding time for yourself in the midst of busy routines.
2. Do not be afraid of controlling demands because of imagined consequences.
3. Sort out the low-priority work and put it aside for later or eliminate it entirely.
4. Put a hold on the seemingly urgent.
5. Find time for yourself and make it a regular part of each day's routine.
6. Encourage others to get to the point on the telephone and at meetings.
7. Respond faster with less formality and more speed.

Chapter 9
Success From Group Effort

1
Time Management and Sports
a. Ineffective time management
b. The ACORN environment

2
Analyzing Time Use
a. Self-evaluation and self-monitoring
b. Personal time management recipes

3
Establishing Direction
a. Setting goals, priorities, and limits
b. Detail management

4
Maintaining Control
a. Active concentration
b. Stress—and distress management

5-9
Time Management Techniques in Practice
Goal Setting (Chap. 5)
Routine Planning (Chap. 6)
Task Orienting (Chap. 7)
Demand Control (Chap. 8)
Limit Maintenance (Chap. 9)

10
Starting and Maintaining Effective Time Management
a. Selecting and using techniques
b. Reaching out to others

DELEGATING RESPONSIBILITIES: ALFRED MYERS

Alfred "Red" Myers has to keep reminding parents he is a volunteer coach. "My family and business come first," Red emphasizes. "Sure, coaching is great fun and I love working with the kids, but it comes third on my list of priorities."

Red also is honest about how much he will attempt as a volunteer baseball coach in a large and highly competitive suburban league. "How some of those others find the time is beyond me. Do they hold jobs during the season?" Red wonders when he hears about the extensive and often complicated programs of rival teams.

As the regional manager for a national oil company, Red has learned much about his own abilities and the consequences of attempting too much. "Our company's success is the result of team effort, not of individuals working alone," Red said. "That message is repeated again and again."

"When I began with the company, I tended to overextend and eventually exhausted myself," Red admits. Luckily, an experienced supervisor decided to help Red out. He required Red to keep a record of how he used his time for a week. The supervisor provided the forms and scheduled a meeting to review them. "At first, I was furious," Red recalls. "With all the work I had to do, my boss was adding one more task of pretty dubious value."

Red stayed angry for 2 days. But on the third day, he took a look at the forms and was stunned at what he saw. "My days were spent trying to do everything myself, which left me with no time to think and organize. I shut out the people available to assist me." The data Red collected the rest of the week only reinforced his initial conclusions, and he discovered that colleagues and his three assistants agreed with him.

Red began to wonder why he had not realized this "loner" tendency earlier. He discussed this with his supervisor who pointed out that as a student and project engineer Red had been judged as an individual, not as part of a group. Until now, Red had never had to depend on others.

Red had to admit his boss was correct. He liked to work alone and was nervous about depending on other people. His parents had always said, "If you want a job done, do it yourself." But in an organization where employees had to support each other to do the work well and on time, that approach was fast becoming impossible.

The need to depend on others and create a team spirit became the foundation for Red's time management program. His personal recipe is based on realistic dependence and the understanding that the load has to be spread out.

DELEGATING FOR SUCCESS

Appropriate delegation is at the heart of Red's time management activities. To prevent personal overloading, he thinks carefully about all the work that needs to be done, then asks himself a few questions to sort things out.

- Is this something only I can do?
- If not, to whom can the work be appropriately assigned?
- Is this person prepared now or does he or she need instruction?

The second key part of Red's time management efforts is ensuring that he has time to discuss what has to be done. Red has learned that it is easier to motivate employees to complete assignments when they know the job's importance and Red's expectations. "I can't be too busy doing my own work or I won't have any time to discuss and explain the job," Red now says.

Red has adopted a few other techniques that reinforce those two basics. His program has taken shape slowly with help from his supervisor and his colleagues' suggestions. In fact, his success at work made Red feel comfortable about responding to an advertisement for volunteer baseball coaches.

Baseball had been Red's sport from the age of 8 through his college years. He played on school teams, Little League teams, and his college varsity squad. In addition to playing, Red had always wanted to coach.

"I just knew working with youngsters would be enjoyable," Red says. "And it has been with the kind of limits and self-management that prevents coaching from becoming a physical and mental drain."

All Red has done is apply the time management program which proved so successful in business to his work as a volunteer coach. "Everyone associated with our team feels better staying inside some clear boundaries," Red reports. "The kids know they will learn and enjoy the sport without crazy pressure to win from me."

Coaching continues to be fun for Red because he sees the team as an organization to be managed intelligently. He remains committed to doing a good job with assistance from others. "We all are volunteers and have many other responsibilities," Red emphasizes. "The team knows this and so do the parents. We all agree that setting limits is central to making this experience a pleasant one for everyone."

PROVIDING CLEAR EXPECTATIONS

At work, Red knows how his performance will be judged. His superiors spell out their expectations annually, every 6 months, as well as for shorter periods of time depending upon the project. When he realized that he needed a team to fulfill those expectations, delegating and instructing others became part of his routine.

As a volunteer coach, Red received only general instructions from the league office. He was asked to help the children learn more about baseball fundamentals, to build their self-confidence, to encourage sportsmanship, and to emphasize the importance of playing as a team. "I thought about those requests, who the players would be, the amount of time we would be together, and what we could realistically accomplish," Red reports. "I made sure to identify my business and family responsibilities during the season, too."

Red spelled out his realistic expectations at the beginning of the season. He wrote a letter to parents about what he hoped would happen, putting emphasis on learning, confidence building, sportsmanship, and team spirit. He was careful to leave out any mention of winning. "The players have that so deeply drilled in I wanted to minimize it," Red believes.

Red emphasized he was a *volunteer* coach and would need assistance from parents if the team were to function. He asked for two assistant coaches, a parent to organize transportation to away games, another to keep track of equipment, and a third to organize refreshments.

He also mentioned what the two assistant coaches would do: One was to be responsible for the outfielders, mainly hitting balls to them and supervising throwing and catching exercises; and the second was to help the pitchers and catchers. "All I wanted was two interested parents with enough time to attend practices and games," he points out. "I could show them what to do."

The heart of Red's team management was *logical delegation.* The two coaches had specific and limited assignments. Red and the pitching/catching coach alternated responsibilities. Other parents handled other details. Red was careful to limit what each was asked to do and to provide clear instructions. Getting messages across clearly the first time is a time management technique Red uses on the job with great success. He found it no less valuable as a volunteer coach, working with other volunteers.

"My goal is *first time understanding,*" Red reports. "Most people listen poorly, and unless I organize to compensate for that lack of attention, much of my time can be wasted."

His approach is simple and straightforward in all instructional situations:

- Announce what will be explained.
- Obtain a commitment from the listener to pay attention.
- Explain what must be done.
- Pause to allow time for questions.
- Encourage a trial or practice if applicable.
- Review or reinforce the main points of the explanation.

"Of course, the steps change depending upon the situation, the topic, and the people involved," Red adds. "But the goal of first time understanding remains; it is something I have to plan for." Red claims he gets attention on most occasions—why?—because listeners sense he has thought out the instructions in advance and will not waste their time with unnecessary words.

MONITORING AFTER DELEGATING

Red learned at work that an overcommitted manager has little or no time to monitor a job. By delegating, Red is able to meet with individual employees, check on their progress, and anticipate problems. As a volunteer coach with two assistants, Red uses this same technique. He finds moments at practice and during games to instruct, to encourage, and to correct players.

By taking a few minutes with each youngster, Red believes he can emphasize baseball fundamentals and boost the players' self-confidence. This activity is an important part of his coaching, and something Red enjoys a great deal. He finds those brief individual contacts motivate the youngsters, and he uses them to tell the players how much progress they are making.

This ability to find time for others has increased because Red is willing to delegate, and he more willingly delegates because he finds time to instruct others. The two reinforce each other. Red feels comfortable assigning work to others at work and on the team. He also is more comfortable taking time to plan because his workload is under control.

REGROUPING MENTALLY AND PHYSICALLY

Red used to feel guilty about taking time away from the job. He traced it to a work ethic instilled when he was very young that equated slowing down with laziness. His daily routine did not include time to think and to plan. It was his supervisor who emphasized the need for regular planning. He advised that lack of planning usually meant a lack of thinking.

Red, however, was uncomfortable with the idea of planning. "It seemed so abstract to me," he recalls. "I couldn't attach any immediate outcome to it." At the company's annual managers' seminar, Red heard a speaker discuss how to release creativity. During her presentation, she suggested using a pen and pad to jot down ideas. Red liked this idea; it would give him something visible and concrete, some notes, maybe a plan of action. Red began to use his pen and pad before meetings, practices, or any event requiring thought and organization. He gained so much from this practice that it became a habit.

At work, Red scheduled some time every day to think, to jot down his ideas, in short, to mentally regroup. He would seek out a quiet location, the company library being his favorite. "There, I'm able to calm down, concentrate, and get more done in a short time," Red emphasizes. "Thirty minutes in the library is equal to almost 2 hours in my office."

The 30 minutes of quiet preparation which he found so valuable at work, also became a habit before each practice and game; the results were similarly positive. Those 30 minutes enable Red to know exactly what will be done at each practice. At this time he prepares a brief game plan and makes a list of who will play, what position, and when substitutions will be made. Then he lets the assistant coaches and players know his plans at the start of each session. As a result, not only does his team know what to do, Red finds he is able to concentrate more on the games and practices.

ORGANIZING PAPERWORK

Red's final organizing technique involves collecting necessary information in the same place. At work and at home, he puts papers related to individual activities in separate folders. This method helps him find what he needs and reduces the amount of stored paper.

"If it doesn't fit into one of the files, out it goes," Red says. "I keep only the paper I need."

Red keeps all the papers related to coaching in one spot, and he keeps only what appears absolutely necessary for the team to function. He has three slim folders which he labels, "Practices," "Games," and "Details." If Red cannot make a practice or game, his filing system makes it easy for an assistant coach to find any necessary information quickly. Red has organized practices so the team can continue in his absence.

Red is much calmer with his personal time management program in which success depends in part on working with others rather than alone. Red remembers what life used to be like before he began delegating the workload. Just as he wants to enjoy and to succeed at work, he wants to enjoy coaching, not be depleted by it. He ensures that the responsibilities of running a team are shared evenly and that he spends his time coaching rather than chasing misplaced information.

Do any of the time management techniques used by Red Myers have potential for you? The time management recipe summarized next should help you decide.

RED MYERS' RECIPE FOR SUCCESS

1. Recognize the importance of delegating work.

2. Set limits based on realistic expectations and communicate them to the team, assistant coaches, and parents.

3. Concentrate on getting messages across clearly the first time.

4. Monitor the team's activities and work with individual players.

5. Set aside periods to mentally regroup, to think, and to plan.

6. Ensure that important papers can be located easily and quickly.

Chapter 10
Starting and Maintaining Effective Time Management

1
Time Management and Sports
a. Ineffective time management
b. The ACORN environment

2
Analyzing Time Use
a. Self-evaluation and self-monitoring
b. Personal time management recipes

3
Establishing Direction
a. Setting goals, priorities, and limits
b. Detail management

4
Maintaining Control
a. Active concentration
b. Stress—and distress management

5-9
Time Management Techniques in Practice

Goal Setting (Chap. 5)
Routine Planning (Chap. 6)
Task Orienting (Chap. 7)
Demand Control (Chap. 8)
Limit Maintenance (Chap. 9)

10
Starting and Maintaining Effective Time Management
a. Selecting and using techniques
b. Reaching out to others

ORGANIZING TIME EFFECTIVELY

"I want to be organized, but . . ."

It is so easy to make excuses why it's not possible to manage time. Capable and dedicated coaches who believe this belittle themselves by emphasizing shortcomings rather than successes. On most days, these coaches successfully manage time, using techniques which have become habits for coaches like John Gibb or Sandra Gruetter.

Many coaches successfully manage time on calm days when they take the time to think, to plan, and to act rationally, but on days like Sarah Stiel's Monday or Frank Adams' Thursday, they exhibit mzungu behavior—running around without any well-defined direction. These coaches treat the bad days as evidence that time management techniques are of no value to them.

Effective time managers use their time management habits to manage *every* day. By concentrating on achieving goals, they feel less pressure. Their lives are not free of the unexpected nor flawless, but they treat the periodic days when plans fall apart and priorities change as exceptions. Most of all, they believe in themselves and the value of a few logical methods to manage time.

This chapter will review the steps for starting an effective, personalized system of time management and offer suggestions for maintaining it. To prevent complacency, it is essential to review your skills periodically. As a busy coach, you must be alert to the same ACORN-creating conditions which undermined the programs of Sarah Stiel and Frank Adams.

SELECTING APPROPRIATE TECHNIQUES

No two people approach time management in exactly the same way. Thus, you must identify a few techniques which work best for you. Techniques can be divided into two groups: those which help focus on direction, and those which help control pressure in work and nonwork situations. The five coaches described in the last few chapters regularly used five to seven approaches, about evenly split between the two groups. Experimentation and help from parents, supervisors, and friends led to their choice of methods. From hundreds of techniques, they selected a few which are listed below:

Time Management Techniques for Direction

1. Establishing yearly, 6-month, and 3-month goals and monitoring them regularly

2. Developing a timeline for certain major accomplishments and milestones to measure progress

3. Ensuring consistency between personal goals and coaching goals

4. Planning for each week with an emphasis on high priority work

5. Sharing plans with colleagues; encouraging feedback and assistance

6. Building a filing system based on key activities

7. Preparing a reminder list of necessary details and keeping the list with you at all times

8. Deciding to complete routine tasks quickly

9. Assigning sufficient time to complete important projects before deadlines

10. Segmenting large projects into smaller, more manageable units using the short periods of time available during a busy day to work on these projects

11. Setting and keeping deadlines for yourself and others using reminders for individuals who tend to be late

12. Focusing on one task at a time by mentally establishing successful outcomes and working back to identify the details that lead there

13. Sorting out the low-priority work and putting it aside for later or eliminating it altogether

14. Recognizing the importance of delegating work

15. Setting limits based on realistic expectations and communicating them to the team, assistant coaches, and parents

Time Management Techniques for Control

1. Concentrating on controlling demands and finding time for yourself in the midst of busy daily routines

2. Not being afraid of controlling those demands because of imagined consequences

3. Controlling interruptions honestly by making others aware of your need for privacy

4. Preventing procrastination with mental disciplining cues that encourage starting sooner

5. Patting yourself on the back each day by reviewing accomplishments

6. Organizing your work area to be comfortable but distraction-free

7. Avoiding self-interruptions by locking in with self-directing messages

8. Writing important details and developing reminder files with the details for procedures regularly used

9. Concentrating on getting messages across clearly the first time and encouraging others to get to the point on the telephone and at meetings

10. Slowing down the seemingly "urgent" requests by stopping to think before responding

11. Finding time for yourself and making it a regular part of each day's routine

12. Responding faster, with less formality and more speed

13. Setting aside periods to mentally regroup, to think, and to plan

14. Being sure that important papers can be located easily and quickly; throwing out irrelevant items

15. Slowing down when you feel pressure and thinking about your priorities

Use these lists and any other ideas you noted from previous chapters to develop your own unique program for managing time. First, identify which techniques you already regularly use. Note why you use them. Do you develop written plans each week? Do you share them with everyone in your program? A plan can guide your action and limit your activities. Do you try to get away to think and to plan for a period each day? With a list of what already works, you can begin to determine if any additional techniques should be incorporated into your daily time management.

As you consider adding new techniques, keep in mind that many techniques require a behavioral change. Old behaviors do not change easily. Coaches who experience most success in improving their time management skills usually begin by selecting four to six techniques for an initial trial. They ask the following questions about each technique:

- Will the technique be immediately useful?
- Am I clear about how to use it?
- Will this technique require me to change my work habits a great deal?
- Will this technique fit into my organization and be accepted by others on whom I depend?

Answering the first two questions should be easy. Most techniques you choose can be useful almost immediately. All that is required is some simple reorganization. How to use the technique should also be clear. You may decide that maintaining a log or a detailed daily planner is just too complicated and time-consuming.

The last two questions need more thought. Small habit changes which lead to improved time use are possible. Individuals who adopt new habits report slight modifications in time management. For example, a person may plan for a longer period of time, organize files differently, set aside more time for thinking, or reduce the number or length of meetings. If change of habit requires too much trouble and too much thinking, success is less likely. Therefore, think about modest rather than major changes.

How the organization and its members accept a new approach should be your next concern. I remember a manager who badly wanted to close his door to have more privacy. He neglected to think about the "open door" tradition and why it was established. That tradition, the manager later found out to his embarrassment, was to encourage managers and staff to exchange ideas freely. Closing the door was an indication to others that he did not want to talk or to receive their opinions.

Privacy is pleasant and necessary. All individuals should enjoy it and respect the need of others to work alone. Unfortunately, there are some organizational traditions which make privacy difficult. By selecting an inappropriate technique, this manager embarrassed himself and probably felt less able to manage his time.

Selection is critical: choose slowly and carefully. Write down your initial choices and let them sit for a day or two. Ask your colleagues for their opinions of the choices. Some techniques will not affect others in the organization: Using lists or arranging files affect only the user. However, priority-setting or interruption-control methods definitely do have an impact, and you are well-advised to obtain reactions before trying techniques which could prove embarrassing.

USING YOUR NEW TECHNIQUES

Once satisfied with your selection of time management techniques, you should make any necessary modifications to your index card reminders. Remember to leave these cards in visible places at home and work so you are constantly reminded of your goals.

Then, check the value of your techniques each day during the first 2 to 3 weeks of use by responding to the following questions:

- Do the techniques blend easily with your daily routine?
- As a result of using these techniques, do you feel more organized and productive?

- Are you starting to modify one or more of the techniques to suit your style and routine?

- Is it becoming easier and more natural each day to employ one or more of them?

With this evaluation, you can discard those techniques which seem more bothersome than helpful. As you review the value of your techniques, you should begin to notice an improvement in your ability to stay on task and to set limits to your daily activities. The habits you will develop include:

- Assessing if you have set aside *enough* time to plan practices, deciding *when* those times are, and knowing *where* you can best work on this task.

- Setting aside sufficient time for detail management, for example, completing reports, planning trips, and making calls. If you do not leave anything to chance, you will not find "minor details" causing major difficulties.

- Reinforcing sound time management habits by seeing how effective they can be. If you look back on a well-organized week, you'll be more willing to focus on high priorities as you plan the next week.

SELF-MONITORING

Reviewing the value of your chosen time management techniques is a valuable first step in determining your progress. However, even after following all the advice and steps listed in this book, remember that it is very easy to slip back into old ways. Our fast-changing and pressure-filled environment often makes the immediate seem more crucial than the truly important. Regular self-monitoring will help you to refocus your attention on goals and to alert you to the need for control.

Periodically, you should analyze your time use in depth. The time charts which were explained in chapter 2 can be used to analyze your daily schedule objectively. These charts will help you identify the source of any specific problems you are experiencing. This information, your own personal observations, and comments you solicit from others in your program will enable you to evaluate fully the success of your efforts to better manage time. Remember this progress review is an inner ring (high-priority) task. It only takes a few minutes and could well become a valued habit.

BELIEVING IN YOURSELF

Self-confidence is essential for successful daily time management. If you believe days cannot be controlled, they will not be. Every example of poor self-organization will be seen as proof you cannot set and keep priorities or complete work according to a schedule. You may subconsciously expect failures and use the all-too-common, "See, what did I tell you!" statement when they occur. Your lack of confidence will affect other people who have to live with your belief that intelligent time use is not possible. You make it easy for them to give up too, perhaps leaving to find a position in a better managed program.

As a coach, you tell your athletes they can succeed. Use the same approach with yourself and time management. Start out in the morning believing you are in charge. You can then plan the day's activities, write out a list, or begin an important project. Remember your *successes*, not your setbacks.

If you lack confidence, use a "proof list" to remind yourself that you do manage time. Look back on what you have accomplished and identify the reasons for these achievements. A list helps boost self-confidence in pressured situations. A sample proof list is shown below. By identifying recent accomplishments and the organizing approaches which made them possible, you will see that success is not due to luck—it depends on intelligent thought and action. To get started, think what you did to finish a recent major project or how you effectively handled routine work.

Proof List

Accomplishment	Organization
1. Finished practice plans, arranged trip to state meet, obtained excellent accommodations	1. Closed door and worked alone for most of Monday morning
2. Turned in reports and travel vouchers	2. Had file on past trips, completed 2 weeks ahead of schedule
3. Completed letter to potential recruits	3. Grouped all routine work together
4. Identified problem team is experiencing with defense	4. Met for 1 hour with coaches on this topic alone; concentrated on that solution alone
5. Found time to develop plan for next game	5. Delegated planning for first two practice sessions to assistant coach

In addition to proving you can manage time, this list will help pinpoint techniques you regularly use to manage time in more tranquil periods. With a sense of what can be done and strengthened self-confidence, you will be better able to build lasting habits that will lead to regular accomplishments and lower distress levels.

STAYING IN CONTROL

Contrast the organization of Sarah Stiel and Frank Adams and the five coaches who used time effectively. Coaches who are good time managers are intent on keeping pressure in check. They are aware of the distress potential in their lives and its negative effects. One of their goals is to control the pace of each day and the forces which can escalate tension levels. They use specific techniques such as stopping to plan action or finding time to relax regularly. Some are able to develop regular concentration routines.

In addition to a mix of personal and professional goals, you must endeavor to stay in control. Remind yourself of this commitment every morning and evening by reviewing to what extent you were successful and why. By identifying the why, you know if slowing down, finding a quiet place to work, or asking visitors to come back later contributes to that control.

Everyone has good and bad days. Unexpected problems increase stress. Sometimes we allow ourselves to be irritated for less rational reasons—an imagined slight from a friend or a line of traffic that doesn't move fast enough can threaten that control. With a commitment to stay in control as much as possible, you begin each day and run your life with a positive "I can and I will" attitude. You also are more likely to know and to use specific techniques that produce desirable levels of control.

Through a sense of control, you increase the likelihood of achieving your personal and professional goals. All time management techniques are related to goals and control. Once you have established goals and are alert to staying in control, consider reaching out to others in your athletic program. As a well-organized leader, you are in position to suggest how intelligent time use can benefit everyone.

CREATING A SANE NON-ACORN ENVIRONMENT

Time is a resource we share with other people. When it is seen as a resource and used intelligently, individuals can work together sanely and harmoniously. In organizations where time is abused, ACORN conditions cause disruption and bad feelings.

As a coach, you should work not only on improving your own time management, but also on influencing how others organize and operate. As your personal recipe takes shape, share its components with others in the program and explain your reasons for using certain techniques. This step tells them you are attempting to improve in ways that will be personally and organizationally beneficial.

Your honesty can begin other activities which can lead to both individual and group improvements in time management. The success of these steps depends upon your active involvement and leadership. When managers of organizations request time management seminars for their staff and do not attend themselves, a major problem that frequently emerges is manager disorganization. Managers who are organized strive to create and maintain well-organized environments. They are concerned others use time intelligently and do not assume rational time use will occur. These managers actively work with all employees to foster improved individual and group time management.

As your time use improves, you can begin to reach out in the following ways:

1. *Identify program directions to athletes, parents, assistant coaches, and support staff.* When they know what is expected of them, their willingness to cooperate with you will probably increase. In addition, as you define what is meant by success, an emphasis on just a few activities becomes more logical. Just as you set personal limits, you are encouraging them to do likewise. Through regular contact and discussion, you can clarify and redefine directions. When directions remain clear and individuals know their responsibilities, enthusiasm to complete assignments is increased.

2. *Help create conditions where concentration and its important benefits are more likely.* By reducing the frequency of dropping in on others, or more emphatically, encouraging assistants to close a door, you build an environment free of constant interruption. You may also want to try cancelling unimportant meetings or limiting their length to a productive hour. Through these and related actions, you will give others an opportunity to concentrate and to avoid ACORN tendencies.

Discussing how group time can be employed more effectively may lead to traditions everyone values. "Leave me alone time," a 30-minute period in which individuals are to work alone twice each day is one method that is used in several public and private settings. Another is "to-the-point" short meetings where the agenda is announced before discussion begins. Reports that are shorter rather than longer is another tradition emerging from group examination of how time should be spent profitably. As a final step, you can encourage athletes to manage their time effectively.

3. *Encourage athletes to manage time.* A time-sensitive coach will help athletes use their time effectively. Set an excellent personal example and emphasize how organization is important in achieving success. Then suggest appropriate time management techniques to athletes, depending upon their age and your contact with them.

Some coaches regularly discuss goals with their athletes. They mention the importance of these goals before the season and help individuals set their own targets. Then during the season, they emphasize setting limits on activities beyond studies and the sport itself.

Other coaches encourage athletes to improve study skills by setting aside specific times and places for these activities each day. A basketball coach reported that her athletes were required to study at certain times while the team was traveling. These examples are just a sample of the kinds of support you can provide to athletes.

Much of your effort is aimed at helping athletes to reach their potential. Better time use is just another way for that potential to be realized. Logical suggestions combined with regular reminders are two ways you can assist athletes to develop sound self-organizing habits.

EPILOGUE

To be successful, you must believe in the value of your efforts. Effective management depends on your willingness to establish direction and to create conditions for achievement. A confident person will set goals and organize the time necessary each day to achieve them.

The second ingredient necessary for success is memory. Remember that we all are prone to allow ACORN conditions to develop. As a busy and energetic coach, you are likely to have many demands on your time. Remembering what can happen when time management is allowed to slip should help you emphasize the importance of sound habits.

Memory is also helpful on hectic and crisis-filled days when you begin to feel organizing just is not possible. Treat those days as exceptions; if you allow ACORN tendencies to take hold, they can become the rule. Remembering that you are a sound time manager most days will help you through the difficult ones. You will not be tempted to toss aside useful approaches because they were not appropriate on a few occasions.

Regular self-reinforcement is the third necessary ingredient. You should evaluate what a few sound time management habits produce. They probably will enable you to establish and reach your goals and to keep daily pressures under control.

Do not expect to change a great deal. Remember, you will have to mold any new ideas to your existing behaviors. By understanding how effectively you currently use your time, and perhaps adding a few carefully chosen new techniques, you will feel productive and in control. Apart from this, there is not much more you can or should do.

Further Reading

A number of books on each of the topics covered in this book are available. The following list includes those which are particularly valuable:

ON TIME MANAGEMENT

Strongly recommended for its wide range of ideas is Alan Lakein's short paperback text *How to Get Control of Your Time and Your Life* (New York: Wyden, 1973). This contains hundreds of specific techniques ranging from common sense to the nearly ridiculous.

R. Alec MacKenzie is another expert on time management. The *Time-Trap* (New York: McGraw-Hill, 1972) is MacKenzie's major effort. Containing many case studies, this book is oriented to executives in public and private organizations. *Time-Trap* emphasizes how a manager with some control over time can bring order to a busy life. An excellent chapter on working with one's secretary to manage time more effectively is also included.

Three books have been specifically directed toward women. Donna Goldfein's *Every Woman's Guide to Time Management* (Millbrae, CA: Les Femmes Publishers, 1977) covers all facets of personal and professional life. Useful organizing routines for the home, office, kitchen, and other areas are presented. Pat Roessle Materka's *Time In, Time Out, Time Enough* (Englewood Cliffs, NJ: Prentice-Hall, 1972) goes a step further in complexity by introducing systems to control time, such as ways to get help from spouse and children. Stephanie Winston's *Getting Organized* (New York: Warner Books, 1978), deals with organizing one's home for more effective operation.

Three other books provide some useful ideas, but are fairly complex, including a number of charts and guides.

Douglass, M.E. & Douglass, D.N. (1980). *Manage your time, manage your work, manage yourself*. New York: AMACOM.

Ferner, J. (1980). *Successful time management—A self-teaching guide.* New York: Wiley.

Rutherford, R.D. (1978). *Administrative time power.* Boulder, CO: Keneric.

If you would like to learn more about your time use personality, information is available from:

Institute for Personality and Ability Testing
PO Box 188
Champaign, IL 61820

IPAT is the publisher of *Timeline*, a customized time management program that I helped to develop.

ON CON-CENTRATION

Two books on this subject are particularly notable. Robert M. Nideffer and Roger C. Sharpe's *Attention Control Training* (New York: Wyden Books, 1978) provides an in-depth description on how mind control heightens concentration. Exercises you can use to increase your ability to concentrate are included.

Terry Orlick's *In Pursuit of Excellence* (Champaign, IL: Human Kinetics Publishers, Inc., 1980) provides suggestions for developing inner motivation. Orlick identifies how to use psychological tools such as relaxation, mental imagery, concentration, and self-control.

Two other books which examine how to self-motivate and concentrate in athletic and nonathletic situations include:

Gallwey, W.T. (1974). *The inner game of tennis.* New York: Random House.

Adams, J.L. (1979). *Conceptual blockbusting. A guide to better ideas.* New York: W.W. Norton & Company.

ON DISTRESS MANAGEMENT

A growing number of books are devoted to this subject. Some treat distress management directly and others emphasize how an individual can build self-confidence and increase personal control over potentially tension-causing events.

Benson, H. (1976). *The relaxation response.* New York: Avon.

Dyer, W. (1976). *Your erroneous zones.* New York: Avon.

Dyer, W. (1979). *Pull your own strings.* New York: Avon.

Ellis, A., & Harper, R.A. (1975). *A new guide to rational living.* North Hollywood, CA: Wilshire.

Harper, R., & Lewis, D. (1977). *Thrive on stress: How to make it work to your advantage.* New York: Warner.

Selye, H. (1975). *Stress without distress.* New York: Signet.

Sperry, L., Mickelson, D.J., & Hunsocker, P.L. (1977). *You can make it happen—A guide to self-actualization.* Reading, MA: Addison-Wesley.

References

Bergeron, T.D., & Wilson, H. (1985). *Coaches guide to sport injuries*. Champaign, IL: Human Kinetics.

Christina, R.W. (1985). *Coaches guide to teaching sport skills*. Champaign, IL: Human Kinetics.

Csikszentmihalyi, M. (1977). *Beyond boredom and anxiety*. San Francisco, CA: Jossey Bass.

Martens, R., Christina, R.W., Harvey, J.S., Jr., & Sharkey, B.J. (1981). *Coaching young athletes*. Champaign, IL: Human Kinetics.

Index